GAUDÍ
The Life of a Visionary

JOAN CASTELLAR-GASSOL

GAUDÍ

The Life of a Visionary

English translation by Paul Martin

Edicions de 1984
Barcelona, Catalonia

Original title:
Gaudí, la vida d'un visionari
© Joan Castellar-Gassol, 1999

Ninth edition: December 2009

Design and illustration: Enric Satué
Photography: Carlos Portrat Díaz and Dani Codina
English translation: Paul Martin

© This edition: Edicions de 1984, s.l.
Pujades, 74-80 - 08080 Barcelona
E-mail: 1984@edicions1984.com
www.edicions1984.com

Printed in Catalonia
Novagràfik s.l.,
Montcada i Reixac

ISBN: 84-86540-55-0
Legal deposit: B. 36.128-2009

INDEX

PART ONE

CHAPTER 1

*The case of the unknown man
knocked down by a tram*

I

A body lay on the blood-spattered stones beside the tram
lines. The wounded person — or was it a dead body? — was
an old man with a full, unkempt white beard. His jacket
and bow tie revealed that he was no working man. But his
clothes seemed to be old. The bottoms of his trouser legs
were frayed, and the soles of his shoes had not been
patched for some time. Perhaps he was a beggar wearing
another man's clothes?

It was mid-afternoon on 7th June 1926, and a number
of passers-by had gathered around the scene of the acci-
dent, in the Gran Via, between Carrer Girona and Carrer
Bailén, in the centre of Barcelona. They were saying that a
tram had knocked down the old man, who was still brea-
thing. With some difficulty, he was carried to a clinic three
streets away. He had no identifying documentation. All he
carried was a handful of currants and peanuts in one pocket
of his jacket, and in the other a book, the Gospels.

It seems that in response to the insistent questions of
the nurses he managed to stammer his name, a few minutes before losing consciousness and being transferred by
ambulance to the Hospital of the Holy Cross, a cold Gothic
building in the medieval nucleus of the city. This was where
they brought the wandering beggars, the people without
home or family, the poor.

The name of the patient, if indeed they had understood it correctly, must have meant little to the nurses. But the dying man was identified the next day by the chaplain of the Temple of the Holy Family, friar Gil Parés: the unknown casualty was none other than the architect Antoni Gaudí i Cornet, the visionary designer of the unfinished Temple itself.

As a result of the impact of the tram, two days later, at around 5 p.m., Gaudí died in the cold iron bed of a shabby room in the hospital for the poor. The only ornament in the anonymous room was a simple print of the Virgin Mary and a few black rosaries hanging from the wall.

Gaudí was almost 74 years old, and he left no descendants. In the last years of his life, the architect had dedicated himself in heart and soul to the construction of a kind of cathedral for the 20th century, an extraordinary Expiatory Temple, that of the Sagrada Família (Holy Family). And he had done so in ever more difficult conditions, surrounded by the indifference of some, the silent admiration of others, the criticisms of the artists considered 'modern' and the ferocious satire of the newspaper cartoonists.

According to the eminent Catalan writer Josep Pla, then a well-known journalist, "Gaudí had enjoyed great fame, but his work on the Temple of the Holy Family was progressing amid great controversy. In many sectors of the intellectual life of Barcelona, it was the subject of permanent criticism."

Known popularly, and sometimes disparagingly, as the 'cathedral of the poor', the Temple of the Holy Family was rising up from the ground little by little, thanks to the donations of the devout. The architect himself had declined to receive any fee, and he himself was one of the helpers who appealed for donations. Josep Pla wrote, "At the end, Gaudí truly was a poor man, and moreover, he looked the part."

But Gaudí's burial, on Saturday 12th June, shook the city of Barcelona like an explosion in an empty vessel. A profound silence invaded the Catalan capital. As the black hearse, drawn by black horses, bore the deceased towards the crypt of the Sagrada Família to be buried, more and more people from the popular classes flocked to their balconies strewn with damasks and black ribbons.

The journalist of the Barcelona newspaper 'La Vanguardia' commissioned to cover the funeral filled an entire page with small print, but lacked adjectives to describe the profundity of the mourning. He limited himself to saying five times that the burial was 'moving'.

III

That summer of 1926, a small man with the glasses of an intellectual, the Japanese professor Kenji Imai, was making a long and arduous journey by sea and train from the Land of the Rising Sun to Europe. It was his first visit to the 'old continent', and his sole interest was to meet three men in person, only three, whom he considered leaders in European architecture: Ostberg of Sweden, Steiner of Switzerland ... and Gaudí.

Telegraph communications sometimes took days to reach travellers, and the fever for speed and haste had not yet overtaken the world. The fact is that, on arriving in Barcelona from his long pilgrimage, Professor Imai was to learn that the venerable Antoni Gaudí had died shortly beforehand. Professor Imai, alone and shaken, went to visit the grave of his admired master, sunk underground in the crypt of the Sagrada Família, and later he wrote:

"It was a rainy day and the workers were sculpting mysterious shapes in the stone. One worker led me to the crypt, a melancholy place diffused with a dim light. Outside, the ivy and the wild grasses grew between pieces of capitals and other shapes sculpted in stone. I looked up and saw the word 'Hosanna'[1] at the top of the tall towers ... with my heart suddenly saddened and darkened by sorrow, I came away."

1.   Hosanna: 'Save me, Lord!'. A Hebrew expression also used in the Christian liturgy.

CHAPTER 2

Origins

I

The surname Gaudí has been established in Catalonia since the 17th century, but its etymological roots must be sought beyond the Pyrenees. In the 5th, 6th and 7th centuries, in Lombardy and other regions of Italy there appears the personal name Gaudens or Gaudenci. It seems to be of Latin origin, and was borne by several ecclesiastical figures, some of whom figure in the Christian martyrological calendar. In fact, one of these gave his name to the town of Saint Gaudens in the South of France.

Whatever its etymological origin, the fact is that the name Gaudí, the Catalan form of Gaudy or Gaudin, is a typical surname of the central and southern parts of France and of the French-speaking part of Switzerland. It is also found in Normandy and southern Belgium.

There are numerous historical testimonies of notable French figures bearing this name, such as the grammarian Jean Gaudin, born in Poitiers in 1617, or Michel-Charles Gaudin, a Minister of Finance under Napoleon, born in Saint-Denis in 1756. Marc-Antoine-Augustin Gaudin, born in Saintes (Poitou) in 1804, was one of the most prestigious physicists of his time. In the 18th and 19th centuries there emerged a family of stained glass artists with the surname Gaudin.

Francophone Switzerland was the homeland of the eminent botanist Jean-François Gaudin (Longirod, 1766), of the writer Jean-Aimé Gaudy-Lefort (Geneva, 1773), and of the naturalist Charles-Théophile Gaudin (Lausanne, 1822). The history of German literature also records the existence of Franz-Bernhard, Baron of Gaudy, apparently born in Frankfurt an der Oder in 1800.

II

For centuries, the predominant tradition in Catalonia was for a person to use only one surname, that of the father, as in Britain, France and most other European countries. In the kingdom of Castile, on the other hand, a different tradition has historically prevailed, and has long been a law of the Spanish State: that of using both the paternal and maternal surnames, in that order.

For this and other circumstances, after Catalonia came under Spanish domination, it became customary to use the paternal and maternal surnames, separated by the word 'i' ('and'). Nowadays in Hispanic publications, the architect of the Sagrada Família tends to be referred to by his two surnames, Gaudí i Cornet.

However, aside from customs and systems of naming, we must refer here to Gaudí's maternal lineage for genetic reasons. The laws of heredity, combined with genealogical research, personal observation, popular wisdom and even common sense, reveal that the heritage of the maternal branch of the family can be equally or even more determining in an individual than the paternal influence.

Both the etymology and the history of the Cornet lineage are well known. The Catalan word *cornet* derives from the Latin *cornetum* and means a place with an abundance of *corners*, a type of bush that grows commonly in oak woods.

In the town of Igualada, in central Catalonia, there is documentation from the mid-14th century of a family called Cornet with a house in Carrer de l'Argent. We know that the paternal ancestors of Antònia Cornet, Gaudí's

16

mother, came form Cal Cornet, a house in the small village of Sant Gallard, situated near the town of Santa Coloma de Queralt, some 30 kilometres from Igualada. Set in the shelter of a hill, the ruined nucleus of Sant Gallard surrounds a small Romanesque church devoted to a curious dedication: Our Lady of the Milk. It currently forms part of the diocese of Tarragona. Cal Cornet is a sturdy house with two storeys and a loft, with a double-slope roof, standing right opposite the church. The few inhabitants of the surrounding area say they have always seen the house closed up.

The village of Sant Gallard belongs to the municipality of Les Piles in the administrative district of La Conca de Barberà. If it has any distinctive peculiarity, it may be this: there is probably no travel agency that can tell you where Sant Gallard is and how to get there.

CHAPTER 3

The saga of the coppersmiths

I

The cradles of great men are often found in modest homes.
Gaudí was born into a long line of artisans. Gaudí's first
paternal ancestor documented in Catalonia is Joan Gaudí,
a young emigrant from the Auvergne in southern France
who in the 1630's was making his living as a travelling
merchant in the Camp de Tarragona region. The parish
archives show that Joan was the son of Antoni Gaudí and
Joana, inhabitants of a small village beside the river Siula
('Sioule' in French) near the city of Clermont-Ferrand.

The Auvergne belonged to the then Kingdom of
France, but its people spoke not French but Occitan, the
language which was used by the Provençal troubadours of
the 11th and 12th centuries and which would later be used
in the 19th century by the Provençal writer Frederic
Mistral, who won the Nobel Prize for Literature in 1905. It
was, and is, a twin sister language of Catalan, with which
it shares the same ethno-linguistic stem. Many Occitan and
Catalan surnames are identical.

During the 16th and 17th centuries, the majority of the
centres of population subject to the Kingdom of France
suffered continual disturbances and tribulations. Firstly,
due to the expansionist wars of the monarchy. Secondly,
due to the brutal wars of religion between Catholics and
Protestants. Wars and famine caused waves of emigration
from the South of France to the other side of the Pyrenees.

Most of the emigrants headed for Catalonia, which at that time was under-populated and had a single dominant religion, the Roman Catholic Church.

Around 1650, about fifteen per cent of the inhabitants of the Principality of Catalonia were Occitan immigrants. Many of them were tradespeople, others were shepherds, and some, like the young Joan Gaudí, had to seek out a living as travelling merchants.

This was an arduous occupation, exercised by young men who did the rounds of the villages and farmhouses on foot, shod with rope-soled sandals, in rain or shine, with their bundles of clothes and cooking utensils over their backs. On arriving at a village or a farmhouse, they announced themselves with the characteristic cry of "Marxant, dones!" ("merchant, women!"). This call became so popular it turned into a nickname: in Igualada there is still a house known as 'Cal Marxant-Dones'.

The uncertain itineraries of the travelling merchant led young Joan Gaudí to Riudoms, a parish in the Camp de Tarragona, which at that time had perhaps less than a thousand inhabitants. There, in 1634, he married Maria Escura, who was also of Occitan origin. In the past, in rural life, weddings tended to be celebrated in the village of the bride.

II

The majority of Joan and Maria's descendants were farmers, but the future architect Antoni Gaudí was born into a long line of coppersmiths, on both sides of the family. In 1843, his father, Francesc Gaudí, born in Riudoms in 1813, the son and grandson of coppersmiths, married Antònia Cornet, who was likewise the daughter and granddaughter of coppersmiths.

It was a good trade, in which the craftsmen maintained the spirit of the guild and a certain endogamy. There work was to make cauldrons from copper or iron for heating or boiling water — no Catalan farmhouse kitchen was complete without its hearth with the cauldron or *caldera*, large or small, hanging from a chain. They also made the *calderó*, a long-handled pot used by shepherds and housewives to take water from the well. Priests, too, often used the *calderó* for sprinkling holy water. Another product of the coppersmiths were the stills and other utensils for making *aiguardent* (liquor): at that time there were many vineyards in the Camp de Tarragona, and the production of *aiguardent* brought prosperity to the town of Riudoms and the city of Reus.

III

In the new Gaudí-Cornet home, fate initially brought the couple more tears and sorrows than joys. Two children died at an early age. But it is written that "There is a time to weep and a time to rejoice, a time to grieve and a time to dance." And the last child, Antoni Gaudí i Cornet, the son, grandson and great-grandson of humble coppersmiths, was destined to survive his parents and to capture the imagination of the five continents.

CHAPTER 4

The garden of the seven secrets

I

Antoni Gaudí was the fifth and last child of Francesc Gaudí, a coppersmith from Riudoms, and Antònia Cornet, from a family of coppersmiths established in Reus. Their first child was a girl called Rosa, who soon manifested a weak constitution. A second girl, called Maria, died at the age of four and a half. Three months later the third child, a boy baptised Francesc, died at the age of two. The fourth, a boy who was also named Francesc, was to be the parents' great hope for the future of the family, but this too was to be cut short. The fifth child, christened Anton, also showed sickly tendencies from an early age.

In the mid-19th century, the deaths of infants were still common in most European homes. However, for a couple to suffer for four of their five children was not common; and it is easy to imagine the cloud of pessimism which must have hung over the Gaudí-Cornet home during the early infancy of their last child.

II

It has not been possible to find in the official archives any document certifying the house and the exact place of birth of the future architect, but the two homes of the Gaudí family in Riudoms are well-known and still standing: a house with party walls in the centre of the town, and a cottage on the farm called Mas de la Calderera outside the urban nucleus. In the city of Reus, the Cornet family had two houses, also with party walls.

According to the Board of the local association 'Friends of Gaudí' of Reus, the future architect was born in a single-storey house at number 4 of Carrer de Sant Joan of that industrious city. Unfortunately, the house was demolished some time before 1903 and replaced, along with other adjoining houses, by a four-storey building which by the mid-1950's belonged to the Banco Hispano Americano.

Nevertheless, the archives of the parish church of St. Peter of Reus contains the deed of baptism. The entry is written in Catalan, and in essence it reads as follows: *"At the baptismal fonts of the parish church of St. Peter the Apostle of Reus … was solemnly baptised Anton Placito (or Plàcid) Guillem, born yesterday at half past nine in the morning, the son of Francesc Gaudí, a coppersmith, of Riudoms, and Antònia Cornet, of Reus, being husband and wife. Paternal grandparents: Francisco Gaudí, a coppersmith, of Riudoms, and Rosa Serra, of Reus. Maternal grandparents: Anton Cornet, a coppersmith, of Reus, and Maria Bertran, of Tarragona. Godparents: Placito (or Plàcid) Gaudí, a turner, of Riudoms, and Raimunda Gaudí, of Barcelona."*

In Catholic countries in those days, children were baptised shortly after birth, and Catalonia and Spain were no exception. And as at that time the deed of baptism served as the birth certificate, we can consider ourselves satisfied with these details and move on to other matters.

III

The Gaudí-Cornet family now had their home and copper-smith's workshop in the city of Reus. From there to the village of Riudoms, where they still had a house and land, was an hour on foot. From the centre of Riudoms to the

Mas de la Calderera farm was a further half hour. During the rains of autumn and winter, the farm was often cut off between a torrent and a brook, but in good weather and at harvest time the path was an easy walk.

The land of the farm, planted with vines, had an area of about a hectare. In the centre stood the cottage, as austere as many others of the outskirts of the town. The bottom storey, with its untiled earth floor, was used as a stable and toolshed. A narrow, hazardous stairway led up to an upper floor with no dividing walls, which was used as a hay loft but had also served as a bedroom. The marks of leaking water were visible: the Arab tiles of the roof had gradually lost their orange colour and there was probably more than one broken. There was no kitchen; the family cooked over a fire outside and ate there too.

In the summer the farm had to be treated for mildew, which attacked the vines and the grapes. In September, at harvest time, many hands were needed for picking the grapes, and no doubt all the family was there working.

Little Anton (the family's affectionate form of his name) spent many periods at the farm, some of them longer than planned. His mother was only able to wean him quite late, and his physical growth proved difficult. At the age of five he began to suffer severe pains that prevented him from walking. The doctors' diagnosis was clear: articular arthritis.

Sometimes when he was unable to walk, they sat him on a donkey and led him around the vineyard. Other times, by the chicken coop, he would amuse himself with pebbles and canes, or catch lizards or study the many kinds of insects that lived around the farm. And so, instead of playing and running around the field like his older brother, Francesc, or working and helping his parents as his sister Rosa did, Antoni Gaudí, as an infant and later as an adolescent too, began to see the world with different eyes from his peers.

The Earth was a strange and uncomfortable habitat, but his parents' farm and the fields surrounding it had become the Garden of the Seven Secrets. There, spiders were master builders who constructed bridges over rivers. Flowers emerged from holy chalices. The shells of snails had fascinating spiral shapes. The poppies in the fields grew in spiral shapes, too. Snakes curled up into spirals to sleep under the stones. The rough trunks of the olive trees also twisted themselves into spirals. Spirals were the ribs and skeleton that supported the world. The smaller lizards were imps that hid in holes in the wall, and the larger ones were dragons from bottomless caverns.

The chimneys of the roofs and of the farmhouses were armoured warriors from another galaxy. The canes were lances, and the palmetto leaves were shields. The humble shepherds' huts, built stone on stone, were sumptuous mansions. And from the great inclined trunks of the carob trees there emerged an immense canopy of branches, and the ancient trunks of the sacred trees were the columns of the Temple.

CHAPTER 5

Chimneys and belltowers, or the three romantics

I

Smoke belched from the chimneys of the red-brick factories. The horses that pulled the big carts loaded with barrels neighed and whinnied. The drivers whipped and cursed their animals. In the mid-19th century, Reus was the second biggest city in Catalonia in number of inhabitants — almost 27,000 — and a bustling industrial and commercial centre of southern Europe.

English merchants had set up shop in the city in the 18th century and had contributed to giving it international fame. The prices set by Reus were taken into account on the international exchanges, along with those of London and Paris. The factories spun cotton and silk, and the production and export of liquor had continued since the Middle Ages. It was precisely the distilling of *aiguardent* in ·stills that provided work for craftsmen such as coopers, coppersmiths and boilermakers. In addition to stills and boilers, Francesc Gaudí, the father of the future architect, made in his workshop the copper pipes that were built into the stills. The pipes are twisted into the form of a snake, and for this reason are called serpentines. Geometers see merely a spiral or helicoidal shape; but children's imagination, and folk memory, have always seen the discomforting form of the snake.

Stills and serpentines were twin implements to those used in the Middle Ages by the alchemists who sought to turn lead into gold. The alchemists' quest failed. But one no less fabulous attempt had succeeded: that of transforming the insipid sugary liquid of the flesh of the grape into a fiery beverage which, if drunk to excess, conjured up visions. Dazzled by this discovery, the ancients called it, in Latin, *aqua vitae*, the 'water of life', and the Catalans called it *aiguardent*, literally 'burning water'.

The coppersmiths and boilermakers made no secret of their work. But the fact is that the serpentines have always attracted the curiosity of nosy parkers, lovers of the esoteric and tax collectors. And just as sandal-makers, cobblers and carpenters worked in full view of everyone, the makers of serpentines plied their craft in the darkness of their workshops.

There can be no doubt that the young Antoni Gaudí spent many hours at his father's side, watching him work or helping him in simple tasks during his healthy periods. In the evening, in the glow of the crucibles and the lanterns, the shadow of the serpentine was projected onto the beamed ceiling. The slightest breath of air over the crucible flame, or the least movement of the craftsman's hand, would cause ripples in the enlarged shadow at the back of the workshop. As silent as the snake itself, the shadow would creep along the walls, where there hung a multitude of tools: mallets, cleavers, punches, clamps, files, gauges, pincers, copper wire and sheet and assorted metal fittings. The moving image of the snake, the most accursed of all beasts, the image associated with the mythological dragon, floated in the darkness.

In the metallic universe of the coppersmith's workshop, peopled with phantasmagorical forms, who knows what visions were to be had!

The craftsmen's livelihood went through good times and bad. In the lean periods, their families had to get ahead as best they could. The story goes that one of the women of the Gaudí-Cornet family often used to visit the house of some well-off neighbours to collect leftover food, old clothes, shoes or small donations.

If they were lucky, craftsmen could finish up with a little property, usually a vineyard or a cottage inherited from their forebears, and with a little money saved, if they had had the help of their children. On the other hand, the possibility of giving them any education beyond primary school never entered their minds. The parents did, on the other hand, try to ensure that their children started to earn a few pennies, and the sooner the better. It seems that Antoni Gaudí, as a boy, started work as a bellows-boy in a factory of cotton yarn and fabrics popularly known as the Vapor Nou (the New Steam Company).

Dressed in a black smock down to his knees and in beaten-up rope sandals, the bellows-boy worked the bellows to blow the fire under the steam boiler. It was not the ideal job for a boy of delicate health who loved the open air, but industrialism was relentless, tireless and heartless.

The conditions inside the factory were brutal, and every day of the week, including Sunday, was a working day. In the Spanish State, to which Catalonia was subject then as now, the law declaring Sunday a day of rest would not be passed until 1904!

But even in the darkest situations a light can appear. It is said that Joan Tarrats, the owner of the Vapor Nou, one day found the young bellows-boy Antoni Gaudí reading a book in a corner of the factory: but instead of telling him off, he asked him what kind of book it was. The boy, rather frightened, told him it was a book of arithmetic. The story was told years ago by Jordi Elias, a student of the life of Gaudí: "Joan Tarrats must have been surprised by the apprentice's interest, and he promised him that the next day he would bring him a book that he would like even more. Perhaps the owner glimpsed an unusual talent in the boy and saw that this talent would be wasted in the factory. No doubt he spoke to the father to recommend that the boy should study..."

According to Elias, the kind-hearted factory-owner Tarrats must in some way have helped the young Antoni to do secondary studies, and something similar must have occurred with Francesc Gaudí, the future architect's elder brother, who after completing his secondary schooling would study medicine in Barcelona.

It is recorded, however, that the mother of the two boys sold a part of the properties she had inherited from her Cornet ancestors to pay for her younger son's studies. It is reasonable to suppose that if she did this for the younger son, she must also have done so for the elder. In any case, at the age of 11, Antoni Gaudí was able to enter the Escoles Pies, the 'pious schools' run by monks in Reus, which provided free education, being supported by private donations and a contract with the municipal council.

The friars of the Escoles Pies constituted a religious order, founded in Rome in 1600, and the teaching provided by their schools was oriented towards the positive sciences. Destined to the education of the popular classes, it enjoyed a certain scientific prestige both in Catalonia and Aragón and in various countries in Central Europe.

The secondary education of the Escoles Pies taught that the one true religion is the Apostolic Roman Catholic faith. But its geometry was Euclidean; its mechanics, Newtonian; its natural sciences, Linnean. And the opportunity to enter into these worlds of knowledge was a great thing, in those days, for the son of a modest family of craftsmen.

The first years of secondary education at the Escoles Pies cost Antoni Gaudí sweat and tears. He failed a number of examinations and scored low marks in various subjects. He was still subject to rheumatic pains, and his character — independent, withdrawn, stubborn and reflective — was not given to the collective discipline nor the systematic routine of education. His teachers could not have considered him a good student, and his classmates, naturally given to fun and games, could hardly have accepted as one of them this boy who did not enjoy jokes, who went his own way and never participated in the oblivious vacuity of the group.

Neither the school nor the atmosphere of the city attracted the young Gaudí. But the law of selective affinities led him to forge firm friendships with two classmates who stood out above the general mediocrity: Josep Ribera, who was Gaudí's own age, and Eduard Toda, three years younger.

Ribera was from Tivissa, a walled town set on a hill in a landscape of carob trees and ancient stones. He lost both his parents when he was fifteen. He was a slim boy with deep-set eyes who composed romantic verses.

Toda could not conceal the fact that he came from one of the eminent families of Reus. He had a broad forehead and noble features, and was the author of a historical compilation on the then abandoned medieval monastery of Poblet, which was published when he was only fifteen.

Gaudí's rural ascendancy was evident in his solid build, prominent forehead and cheekbones and large nose. But he was also distinguished from his classmates by his reddish-tinged fair hair, his pink skin and his clear blue eyes. Individuals of these characteristics were not common in the Camp de Tarragona, and it was often said that Gaudí looked like a Scandinavian, a remark that he did not take kindly. As for his inclinations, he drew with ease, had great manual dexterity and observed the details of old buildings as if he were a master builder.

According to the memoirs which Toda published in his old age, "the three friends, outside school, had one common interest: walking in the fields, contemplating ancient remains in the area. In particular they sought out evocative spots which would stimulate their romantic imaginations." Toda said that Gaudí, in particular, felt an attraction for ruined constructions such as some old Roman ovens or a nearby aqueduct.

They once went on an outing to the abandoned monastery of Poblet, situated some 30 kilometres from Reus. Founded in the 12th century, Poblet was an ancient glory of the Cistercian order of monks, which was founded in Citeaux, near Dijon (France) in the late 11th century. The monastery had once been a burial site of kings and saints, but now it was a site of desolation. In 1809, it was sacked by the troops of the French emperor Napoleon Bonaparte, and in 1835 the local anti-clerical militias continued the task of its destruction: having already set fire to a convent in Reus, they threatened Poblet, the friars fled, and the subsequent pillage and the indifference of the local authorities did the rest.

In the idealistic imagination of the three boys, Poblet was the symbol of the ancient glories of History, with an aura of romanticism which turned their gaze towards an idealised vision of the Middle Ages. Now the ivy climbed up the slender Gothic columns of the cloister and crept onto the roof. The ivy veiling the holes in the broken arches let only a dim, greenish afternoon light into the ghostly halls of the building, which was now reduced to a refuge for rats and owls. But to the eyes of an artist, the green-tinted background highlighted, as if in a Turner painting, the stylised beauty of the bright stones in the foreground.

Modern-day society could replace the belltowers with chimneys — but the three romantic students of Reus, and they alone, would return to the ideal medieval age and would restore its lost beauties. They would rebuild Poblet.

For some days in the summer of 1869, the three

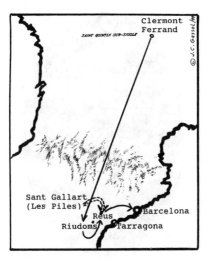

1. Schematic map showing the itinerary of a branch of the Gaudí lineage from the region of Clermont-Ferrand (Auvergne) to Riudoms (Camp de Tarragona). The broken line shows the movement of a branch of the Cornet lineage from Sant Gallard, near Santa Coloma de Queralt, to Reus.

2. Francesc Gaudí i Serra, the father of Antoni Gaudí, in a photograph from 1904, at the age of 91 (photo: archive).

I

3. Rosa Gaudí i Serra, paternal aunt of the architect (photo: archive).

4. Francesc Gaudí i Cornet, the architect's brother, in a portrait from the sheet of photographs of the graduates of the Faculty of Medicine of Barcelona of 1872 (photo: Ferré).

5. The house that belonged to the Gaudí family (marked with a white cross at the base) in the Sant Francesc neighbourhood of Riudoms, in the mid-20th century (photo: Ferré, reproduced in *Defensa de Gaudí* by J.M. Guix Sugranyes).

III

6. The Mas de la Calderera farm outside Riudoms, once the property of the Gaudí family (photo: archive).

7. Excursion of the Catalanist Association of Reus, April 1886, to Salt de Cercós, La Selva and Paret d'Algada (Archives of the Heirs of Pau Font de Rubinat).

8. The architect Antoni Gaudí i Cornet at the age of 26 (photo: Salvador Vilaseca District Museum, Reus).

9. View of the village of Riudoms in the early decades of the 20th century (photo: Roisin, by courtesy of Joan-Ramon Corts, Municipal Archive of Riudoms).

10. View of Sant Gallard. The ancestors of Gaudí's mother came from this small village (photo: Salvador Palau, *el Galo*).

11. Gaudi's family house at Reus, in a photo *circa* 1960 (Photo: Ferré).

12. View of the Plaça de l'Ajuntament of Reus during Gaudí's lifetime (photo: archive).

13. Prim Square at Reus, *circa* 1910 (photo: Archive).

VIII

14. Father Josep Manyanet, originator of the idea of building a Temple of the Holy Family (photo: courtesy of the Congregation «Fills de la Sagrada Família, Jesús, Maria i Josep»).

J.M.J.

Excmo. é Ilmo. Sr. D. D. José Caixal y Estradé,
digno Obispo de Urgel.

Gerona 24 Junio de 1869.

Mi muy venerado Prelado y P. en Cristo:
voy á manifestar á V.E. Ilma un pensamiento, al parecer hermoso y devoto, que me ha ocurrido.

Meditando sobre los males que traen desquiciada la sociedad y sobre su mas oportuno y eficaz remedio, y no hallándolo sino en la unión de todos los Obispos con la Silla de Roma en el próximo Concilio ecuménico; me vino la idea de interesar al glorioso Patriarca S. José en este importantísimo negocio por medio de la erección de un templo expiatorio fabricado por la caridad de los españoles, grabando en su frontispicio para memoria de las generaciones futuras estas ó parecidas palabras: "Al glorioso Patriarca S. José Patron de la Iglesia universal y Restaurador de España"
Para promover defraudadas nuestras esperan-

15-16. Reproduction of the letter written by Father Manyanet to the Bishop of Urgell on 24th June 1869, proposing the building of a Temple of the Holy Family.

ñas, empezaríamos rezando una misa todos los miércoles á S. José, implorando su poderosa protección, y todos los meses otra á María Immaculada para los piadosos fines de los que se dignaran contribuir con sus limosnas al levantamiento de este magnífico templo.

Espero que V. E. Ilma se dignará darme su parecer caso de merecer su aprobación. En caso afirmativo, escusado es decir que se daría exacta cuenta de los ingresos y gastos para que nadie pudiera sospechar de la buena inversión de los fondos.

Saluda respetuosamente á V. E. Ilma su afmo súbdito y humilde hijo en Cristo

Q. B. E. P. A. de V. E. Ilma.

José Mananet Vives, Pbro.

Nota. Este pensamiento lo comuniqué mas tarde al Sr. D. José Bocabella (a) Viuda Pla, de Barcelona, quien lo inició en el Propagador de la devoción á S. José, dando todo esto pie al levantamiento del famoso templo de la Sda. Familia.

17. The Christian bookseller and magazine publisher Josep A. Bocabella, the promoter of the Temple of the Holy Family (photo: archive).

18. The Holy Family, according to a popular print of the beginning of the 20th century (photo: Archive).

19.   Antoni Gaudí, at 36 years of age (photo: S. Vilaseca County Museum, Reus).

XIII

20. Josefa Moreu i Fornells, of Mataró, Gaudí's unrequited love (photo: Moreu family, by courtesy of the Caixa d'Estalvis Laietana).

21. Monastery of Montserrat, 1904. Foreground, sitting on the stones, the doctor Pere Santaló and Rosa Egea, Gaudí's niece; centre, his father, Francesc Gaudí; rear, the architect Antòni Gaudí (photo: archive).

22. Interior of Gaudí's workshop in the Temple of the Holy Family (photo: archive).

23. Sketch of the Temple of the Holy Family, made *circa* 1915.

24. Drawing by Gaudí (photo: S. Vilaseca County Museum, Reus).

Il·lustríssim Sr. D. Joseph Torres y Beges

Barc. 3 juny 1914

Lo nostre amich D. Eusebi Güell
està mal de salut y penso ser el seu estat
de gravetat. parlan de aquesta gravetat
ab el Rnt. M. Gaspar Vilarrubies, me
ha significat tal vegada fora convenient
lo escriure á V. Y., el estat del nostre
amich, com no fuig en lo present, para
dir á V. Y. que M. Vilarrubias y son
servidor estem á la disposició de V. Y. si
creu convenient fer quelcom.
Besant l'anell y demanen la benedicció
J. Y. S. Antoni Gaudí

25. Gaudi's autograph, of the year 1914 (photo: *courtesy of* «*Friends of Gaudí*», *Reus*).

26. Day of Corpus Christi, spring 1924. The traditional pro-
cession leaves the Cathedral of Barcelona. In the foreground,
with black suit and white beard, Antoni Gaudí (photo: Brangulí /
National Archive of Catalonia).

27. Project of the church of the Güell Colony of Santa Coloma de Cervelló (photo: Archive).

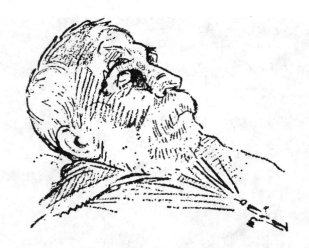

28. Gaudí on his death-bed (drawing by *Renart*).

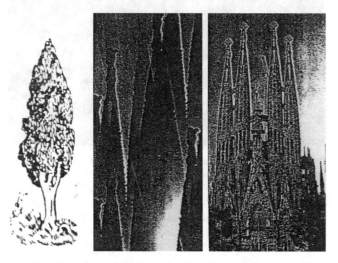

29. The spires of the Temple of the Sagrada Família of Barcelona recall the shape of the cypress tree, an ancient symbol of eternity, Gaudí said «Nature is our great teacher.»

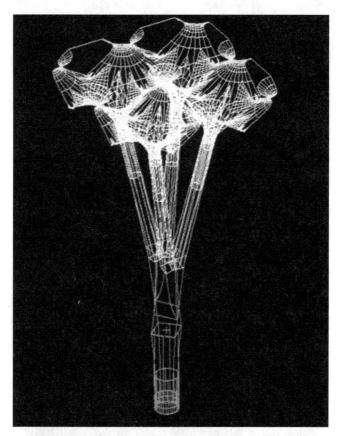

30. Computer simulation of the forms adopted by the elements of the central nave of the Temple of the Sagrada Família, according to a study performed by technicians of Victoria University of Wellington, New Zealand, and of the Polytechnic University of Catalonia. The technicians have confirmed that the architectural forms conceived intuitively by Gaudí and realised by artisanal methods respond to exact mathematical formulas.

31. Bust of Gaudí, by Joan Matamala (photo: Archive).

32. Church of Saint Peter of Reus, where Anton Gaudí was christened (photo: Tourist Bureau or Reus).

33. West façade, under construction, of the Sagrada Família.

34. Structure of the Sagrada Família now finished: 1. Nativity Façade (east). – 2. Passion Façade. – 3. Evangelists' Tower. – 4. Virgin's Tower. – 5. Saviour's Tower. – 6. Sacristy. – 7. Cloister. – 8. Apse. – 9. Doorway of Faith. – 10. Doorway of Hope. – 11. Doorway of Charity.

35. Gaudí was inspired by the strange forms of Montserrat, the holy mountain of the Catalans.

36. Artificial cave conceived by Gaudí and excavated in the mountain of Montserrat, dedicated to the Resurrection of Christ and executed in such a way that when the sun rises on Easter Day its rays reach the back of the cave.

37. Gaudí's dedication to the works of the Sagrada Família in his final years became almost obsessive. He used to eat on this corner table in his workshop at the foot of the building works.

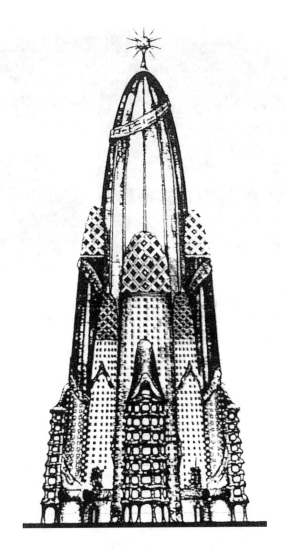

38. Hotel Attraction, in New York, a project sketched by Gaudí in 1908 for a group of American businessmen (drawing by J. Matamala from Gaudí's sketch).

39. Dome of the Palau Güell, close to the Rambla in Barcelona. Gaudí saw it as a symbol of the cosmos.

40. The Teresian Sisters' School in Barcelona, designed by Gaudí in 1889.

romantics moved into the house of one of Ribera's sisters in the town of Espluga de Francolí, half an hour's walk from Poblet. They made an inventory of the books still conserved in the monastery and of the objects belonging to it which had been scattered in different directions. They took measurements of the grounds, made plans for the reconstruction, and calculated in detail the costs of the works. With great foresight — over a century before the arrival of mass tourism in Catalonia! — they imagined that the principal source of revenue would lie in charging the future visitors an entrance fee.

Gaudí, among other things, chose the precise quality of the stone required to rebuild the walls, the vaults and the roofs. "In the studies he made for the execution of the works," said Jordi Elias, "Gaudí arrived at details of an intuition and acuteness which are absolutely astounding for his young age." Gaudí had just turned seventeen, and he had an ideal. This was the time in which a turbulent romantic, the French writer and painter Victor Hugo, was proclaiming, "L'idéal c'est le goût de Dieu" ("The ideal is the taste of God").

PART TWO

CHAPTER 6

The Charisma of Josep

I

During the years when Gaudí was toiling at his secondary studies, a long-lasting disturbance was building up. The events of those times included two or three which, when regarded today from the perspective of a century and a half, are highly evocative.

In principle, they had little to do with the young, unknown student of Reus. Later developments, however, suggested that there was a confluence between the steps taken by Gaudí and the fate of other members of his generation.

The prologue to these events must be sought in Rome, in the year 1861. A group of Catalan pilgrims, which included a bookseller from Barcelona named Bocabella, had just arrived in the city, and the first thing they met with was a guard of soldiers armed with rifles with bayonets attached.

What for pilgrims was the Holy City had continued to be, since before the year 1000, the capital of the Papal (or Pontifical) States, the most influential international organisation which had existed up to that time. But Rome was still to become the capital of the nascent Italian state. For two thousand years the name 'Italy' had been no more than a vague geographical term, such as 'Europe' or 'North America'. But in the early decades of the 19th century, in Turin, Genoa, Milan, Venice and Florence, there had emerged the project of unification of all of these territories into a single state.

The majority of unionists — revolutionaries, anti-clericals, members of secret societies — wanted to create a republic, a concept which in those times was charged with revolutionary connotations. But for fear of alarming France, which was giving them military support, the unionists inclined to unify Italy under the flag of a monarchy which would be little more than symbolic. And to this end they chose the flag of what the historian of diplomacy Charles Petrie called "the insignificant Dukes of Savoy". Half French, half Italian, the Savoys lived in Turin, but Savoy was and continues to be a region of France. A certain Vittorio Emmanuele di Savoia was proclaimed King of the nascent Italian state, in that year of 1861. But the unionists still required to take the last and most symbolic bastion: for the Italy of the lay people to be born, the Rome of the Popes had to die.

II

The definitive fall of Rome was anxiously awaited in Protestant circles and by the rationalist elites of northern Europe, the free-thinkers. In some of these circles, the hostility towards the Papacy was to endure for a long time, and can still be detected today. One example of this is the Free University of Brussels, founded in 1834 by members of the rationalist group Le Libre Examen in order to compete with the Catholic-run University of Liège. The Free University no longer intoned the Latin verses of the *Gaudeamus igitur*, the traditional hymn of the medieval universities of Europe. The new hymn of the Free University, with words in French, was to include a bellicose verse exalting the determination of the valiant students to fight "*contre la Papauté*", against the Papacy.

The great body of Catholicism was worried not only about the destruction of the earthly power of the Popes. The concern was much greater, more varied, more profound.

In the announced annexation of Rome into the lay republic of Italy, some fundamentalist Catholic doctrinarians saw the apocalyptic sign of the Forces of Evil deployed all over the world. Others —high officials, bishops, abbots and canons— saw the loss of their privileges and power. All of them, and even more so the humble friars, the rural priests and the devout believers of the parishes, particularly in Catalonia, feared the advent of new persecutions, new burnings of churches and convents.

The fall of Rome seemed also to be the allegory of the progressive collapse of Christian virtues in the artisan and working-class families. Everyone could see that the de-Christianising tendency was growing inexorably in the big cities. If this phenomenon had been merely of a religious nature, it would only have troubled individual consciences. As it was, its most visible consequences were social.

In the rural world there might be bad blood and domestic dramas, and the journeyman might be treated as a pariah. But religious faith in the home sometimes contributed to maintaining a certain inner peace, the product of an attitude of resignation before the adversities of fate. Despair was more often seen in the homes of the urban proletariat, deprived of the consolation of religion. This is reflected in the novels of Charles Dickens, Émile Zola or Knut Hamsun, who portrayed the wretched existence of working men lying drunk in taverns, ruined by gambling or abusing their wives and children.

In the view of sociologists and rationalist observers, all of this was a consequence of the mechanistic doctrine which herded peasants into the towns, of the Industrial Revolution, of bourgeois exploitation. Some philosophers of history would go further, such as Oswald Spengler, who would say: "We have smelt the devil in the machine and we have not been mistaken. For believers, the machine means the dethronement of God."

III

In the face of the crisis of the Christian family, in the most traditional Catholic circles, the figure of the foremost *pater familiae* of all, Joseph the carpenter, the putative father of Jesus, gradually acquired greater and greater relevance amid the Catholic church's extensive repertory of saints.

In Gothic and Baroque religious iconography, the character of Joseph tended to appear in a discreet secondary position, behind or beside the Virgin and the child Jesus. But by the mid-19th century, in the minds of many simple believers and some religious leaders, Joseph was regarded rather as the head of the Holy Family, and therefore as the model of the head of the household for *all* Christian families.

In Catalonia, the forename Josep was very common. In the past, it had been merely one more of the many Old Testament names borne by Jewish citizens. As late as the 15th century it would have been very difficult to find a Christian inhabitant of Barcelona with the name Josep. Since the 18th century, however, it had become popular among Christian families and vulgarised to such an extent that to this day there still survives the peasants' saying *"De Joseps, Joans i ases, n'hi ha per totes les cases!"* — "in every house there's a Joseph, a John and an ass!".

For this reason, this forename was enveloped in a kind of vague affection in the popular imagination. This was also manifested in the popular consideration of the barefoot Carmelites or Congregation of St. Joseph, introduced into Barcelona in the late 16th century, who were commonly known by the affectionate diminutive of *josepets*.

At the same time, everywhere there abounded initiatives intended to foster the devotion to the Holy Family. Thus, Captain Henri-Hubert Belletable, who died in 1855, had founded the *Association de la Sainte Famille* in Liège, Belgium.

More particularly, it was proposed to exalt the figure of

St. Joseph, whom Pope Pius IX proclaimed Patron of the Catholic Church. It is not unusual that some of these initiatives should originate in persons baptised with the name of Joseph.

A certain Joseph Huguet, for example, a member of the Marian Friars, a congregation with French origins, published in Saint-Foy (Burgundy, France) a magazine entitled *Propagateur de la Dévotion a Saint Joseph.* Inspired by this, another Joseph, Josep Maria Bocabella, the Catalan bookseller who had travelled to Rome in that year of 1861, decided to start a similar publication in Barcelona.

Bocabella, who had lost his own father when young, was a small man with little hair adorning his noble head. His exuberant dark moustache was probably the only concession he made to the fashion of the time. In the portrait of him which still survives, the most remarkable trait is his profound gaze, as if fixed on a world beyond this one. But the facts demonstrate that he was also very down-to-earth. In 1866 he founded in the Catalan capital the 'Spiritual Association of Devotees of Saint Joseph', which became known as the Josephine Association, and its members as *josefins* —and the magazine *El Propagador de la Devoción a San José*, which he disseminated throughout Catalonia, the Spanish provinces and Latin America. The publication met with an unexpected success, gaining almost 600,000 associates in a short period of time.

Meanwhile, Josep Manyanet, a young priest from a poor farming family of Tremp in central Catalonia, who had also lost his father at an early age, founded the congregation 'Children of the Holy Family, Jesus, Mary and Joseph'. This man, with his peasant features and dark, honest eyes, a tireless worker with a quick mind, perhaps never imagined that his congregation would come to have dozens of centres in Europe and America, from Barcelona to Silver Springs (Maryland, USA), as it does at present.

But Friar Manyanet did have a vision of the future. This was no longer the time of the medieval cathedrals. The faith and the finances of the Catholic Church were on the decline. But on 24th June 1869, Friar Manyanet informed his bishop in a letter that he had had an idea: to erect a temple to "the glorious patriarch Saint Joseph" with the alms of the devout. Later Manyanet presented his idea to Bocabella, who in April 1874 expounded it in his magazine. The project seemed by no means easy.

IV

A hundred years later, as the temple proposed by Manyanet and promoted by Bocabella was gradually rising towards the clouds in the city of Barcelona, the journalist Josep Pla, a conservative but a sceptic in religious matters, would say that Bocabella's magazine, "without relinquishing the inevitable weightiness of the time", had been "one of the most enormous concentrations of inanity, cliché and apologetic mediocrity that has ever existed!" He was probably not far wrong regarding the literary style and the indubitable sanctimoniousness of many devotees. But Pla, always the acute observer of external reality, who portrayed with clear lines and broad strokes, failed to appreciate the spiritual background of the matter. And the question was that the devotion to the saints and the belief in their mediation, even though manifested outwardly in an ingenuous or sanctimonious manner, constituted a real force. And the reiterated testimonies of witnesses who swear they have seen apparitions of the Virgin Mary are an intriguing fact.

The English novelist and journalist Graham Greene, who became captivated by these phenomena and converted to Catholicism in 1926, said that in all of these apparitions there was one common trait: the call to prayer. "The message is so simple," said Greene, "that it would seem unimportant to us if we had no notion of the tremendous force of prayer, this mysterious and inexhaustible power which is capable of moving mountains."

These were phenomena for which the rational science of the late 19th century had no explanation. Whether the apparition of the Virgin Mary in 1871 in the grotto in Lourdes (Gascony, France) was truth or imagination, it was a fact, confirmed by agnostic doctors, that there were patients who found a cure there. Some said 'inexplicable', others said 'miraculous'.

Émile Zola, also a novelist and journalist — whose works were proclaimed 'mortal sin' by certain religious figures in Spain after the Civil War — went to Lourdes out of curiosity. He went as a sceptic, and returned testifying that the miracles were true.

Alexis Carrel, the agnostic French surgeon who was awarded the Nobel Prize for Medicine in 1912 and who worked for years at the Rockefeller Institute for Medical Research in New York, witnessed the instantaneous cure of a girl who was dying from tubercular peritonitis. At first, Carrel tried to convince himself that he had erred in his diagnosis. In the end, he declared "I have had the opportunity to observe some completely extraordinary events, which prove that certain phenomena considered the stuff of legends or witchcraft are perfectly real or natural." After his experiences of cures in Lourdes, Carrel converted to Catholicism.

And such inexplicable phenomena did not only occur in Lourdes. In the wretchedly poor village of Knock, in Ireland, one rain-washed, windswept day in 1879, more than fifteen people saw, according to the testimonies of the time, the apparition of the figures of St. Joseph, the apostle St. John, the Virgin Mary, a lamb and a cross, amid a blaze of light above the belltower of the village church.

In the late 19th century, a triumphant scientism was affirming that science was capable of solving all questions. The existence of supernatural events, however, remained evident. The times were ripe for recalling the passage from Shakespeare's Hamlet: "There are more things in heaven and earth, Horatio, than are dreamt of in your philosophy."

And among those things, one was related which has a direct relationship with our story.

It was at the time when Friar Manyanet's idea of erecting a temple to St. Joseph, having been welcomed and disseminated by Bocabella, was beginning to gather force. Donations were being collected, especially from among the humble classes, but still no-one knew when nor where nor how the first stone was to be laid.

We mention this fact here because it was related by a reliable source: Josep Pijoan, a Barcelona architect, who for years was a professor of art history at Pomona College in Claremont, California, and at the University of Chicago. Professor Pijoan, born in 1881, had known Antoni Gaudí personally, and followers of Josep Maria Bocabella had told him, "At that time it was being said in Barcelona, particularly among the *josefins*, that a relative of Bocabella had had a divine inspiration: the architect of the planned temple would have blue eyes!"

Blue eyes? Why?

CHAPTER 7

Barcelona, the great enchantress

I

At the time of the grape harvest in the Camp de Tarragona, in mid-September, the green of the vine leaves would turn to gold in the light of the setting sun. But that September of 1868 was to be unlike all others for Antoni Gaudí.

It was in the middle of the month when the students applied for the renewal of their enrolment for the coming academic year. Gaudí had turned 16 and only had the final year of his secondary education to complete. But how was he to do it?

On 19th September, General Prim, a liberal conspirator of 54 years age, and a native of Reus, had led a rising against the Spanish monarchy. The revolt spread like wildfire through Catalonia and the provinces of the periphery of Spain. In Reus, factories were burned down and the houses of the most eminent bourgeois families were raided. The revolutionary council which took charge of the town proclaimed civil marriage and the dissolution of all religious orders. The monks of the Escoles Pies had to flee from their monastery and abandon the city.

The Gaudí-Cornet family found itself immersed in an uncertain situation. The revolt had aggravated the latent economic crisis. Work was declining. Both parents were now 55, virtually old age by the parameters of the time, and it was necessary for the children to be able to take over the family responsibilities.

45

The parents had little confidence that they could count on their daughter, Rosa, who was now 24. The elder son, Francesc, was expected to become a doctor: everyone knew that he had excellent qualities to achieve this aim. And it seemed that, if all went well, the youngest, Anton, could learn the trade of master builder or at least work as a draughtsman.

Perhaps the solution was to be found in Barcelona.

II

Antoni Gaudí studied the final year of his secondary schooling at an Institute of Secondary Education in the Catalan capital, most probably living with some family acquaintances and returning to Reus the following summer. Having obtained his school leaving certificate, he then returned to Barcelona to prepare to qualify as a master builder, or architect as the profession later became known.

During the academic year, he and his brother Francesc lived in shabby boarding houses. For a while they lived in a house in the Placeta de Montcada, beside the magnificent Gothic church of Santa Maria del Mar. Another time they lived in a dark house in the narrow Carrer de la Cadena near the Rambla.

Their trips home to the family in Reus became less and less frequent. As Gaudí had to work to pay for his studies, he soon began to spend nearly the whole year in Barcelona.

III

A worker's life in Barcelona was hard. The hours in the workshops were endless, both for the craftsmen and their apprentices. In the homes and boarding houses there were always vegetables, bread, and wine, which quickly turned sour; cod and herrings appeared occasionally, but meat only on Saturdays, and then only with a little luck, and it was not the steaks of the rich but the scraps and extremities of pork and beef.

To see the sun through a window was a luxury. People packed into the cramped apartments that were being built. The rural exodus brought the population of the capital to some 300,000, with a density which was double that of Dickens' London. An inspired journalist wrote in a leaflet which was circulating in 1871, "In Barcelona, I see its dirty streets, its shoddily-built houses, its thoroughfares like the chasms where crows make their nests. I see the constriction, the damp ... Where are its gardens? Where are its open spaces? Where are its three-lined parks? Where is modern town planning?"

It was common for poor tenants to sublet rooms to even poorer people in order to make ends meet. Many housewives had to do their washing in the basins in the public squares or on waste land. And the lack of hygiene and the generalised ignorance contributed to the spread of disease. The cholera epidemic of 1865 had caused almost 3,800 deaths, and the yellow fever of 1870 had claimed almost 1,600 victims.

The city ignored the rhythms of nature and its unpredictable demands. One night in the winter of 1862 it began to rain; the following morning it was still raining, and the Rambla, the vital artery of the city running down from the hills to the sea, could no longer evacuate all of the water. The famous Danish children's writer Hans Christian Andersen was in Barcelona at the time, staying in a hotel in the Rambla itself, and he wrote the following account of what he witnessed:

"From my hotel balcony I saw how the cobbled street had become a river, rising and sweeping everything before it. In the past there had been a drainage channel here which led the rising waters to the moat which used to surround Barcelona; but it had been recently filled in with gravel and stones to provide building land for the expansion

47

of the city. So the drainage route was now blocked and the river grew and grew. The flood, roaring like a millrace, tore up trees and shrubs by the roots. Inside the shops, people were wading in water up to their waists. Everywhere there was shouting and screaming ... Later I learned that several people had disappeared down the holes of the sewers ... I would never have imagined the power of a mountain torrent. I thought of the story that could emerge from this normally quiet little mountain stream, lined with aloe bushes and prickly pear plants."

But industrialisation and the frantic pace of commerce did not stop. The city, having swept down its medieval walls, overflowed and spread unchecked, like a stinking oil slick, over the vegetable gardens and fields of the surrounding plain. What the city needed now were bricklayers, plasterers, labourers, carpenters ... builders!

IV

And this was how Antoni Gaudí, having just turned 21, began his career in architecture, working as a draughtsman in a workshop. It seemed he had managed to avoid doing the military service in an infantry regiment for which he was destined. His parents had taken the decision to close down and sell the coppersmith's workshop in Reus and to settle in Barcelona with their sons, who represented the family's future.

For the elder son, Francesc, a brilliant future was expected. On 12th March 1873 he passed his practical examinations for the degree in medicine from the University of Barcelona, but he did not receive his diploma until 22nd November 1875, after paying the corresponding fee — perhaps he had to wait to accumulate the money? He was a very bright young man, with thick hair, clear eyes, large lips and the prominent chin of a strong-willed man, adorned by fashionable long side-whiskers. The distinguished traits of Doctor Francesc Gaudí i Cornet resembled those of his maternal aunt, Rosa Gaudí i Serra, a portrait of whom is still conserved.

On the other hand, the future of the daughter, Rosa, was not at all assured. According to the testimony of an architect who was Antoni Gaudí's assistant, Rosa "got married young and unwisely, to an Andalusian musician called José Egea, a bohemian and a drinker."

The future of the youngest child, Anton, was also unclear, but despite his difficult character he was very determined, original and willing to learn.

Two years passed, and in the summer of 1876, a dark shadow fell over the Gaudí-Cornet household. On 1st July, the recently-qualified doctor in medicine Francesc Gaudí Cornet died suddenly, at the age of 25 years and two months. There is no record of the cause of death. Then his mother fell ill, and two months later, on 8th September, Antònia Cornet also died, at the age of 63, with a profound sorrow in her heart.

PART THREE

CHAPTER 8

Progress

I

In the evenings, in the dim light or by the lamp of his room, Antoni Gaudí recorded in a lined notebook the commissions of work he had pending. They were brief notes, simple utilitary reminders, of telegraphic syntax and untidy handwriting, but on the evening of 25th November 1876 he headed the page with this innocent reflection: "There is a lot of work to do if we are to get ahead."

He was then 24 years old, and undergoing severe troubles. He was still grieving for the recent deaths of his mother and brother, he was still not entirely free from the threat of military service, he had not yet managed to finish his studies, and he had a pile of outstanding commissions that had to be completed one way or another in order for the family to "get ahead".

The many jobs he had taken on in order to pay for his studies and bring money home to his parents' house — which was now only his *father's house* — had distracted him from the obligations imposed by the School of Architecture. Moreover, his own working rhythm was painstaking, thoughtful, detailed, slow. But he had the confidence of a man who knows his worth and knows that others also know it. One way or another, the horizon would open up for him. And sure enough, within two years he had freed himself of his military service, obtained the title of architect and received offers of work from various directions.

George R. Collins, the great American specialist in Gaudí's work, has pointed out that the architect's first commissions after qualifying did not exactly come from clients in the highest ranks of society: the inventor Enric Girosi requested a model of kiosk; the businessman Pau Miró commissioned a wall, the railing and the roof with columns of a theatre in the village of Sant Gervasi (later absorbed into Barcelona); and the glove manufacturer Esteve Comella asked him to design a shop window.

This variety of commissions had an explanation. In certain circles of the building trade, Gaudí had become known as a man of talent: he had not only been an architect's draughtsman, but he was also skilled with his hands and had that rare power of imagination typical of self-taught inventors.

II

Within the old enclosure of the city walls of Barcelona, there were workshops of experienced craftsmen. In one of them, belonging to a sculptor called Llorenç Matamala, the young student Gaudí had learned to make models from plaster or clay, both of statues and of varied items of decoration commissioned by builders. In the adjoining workshop, belonging to an Eudald Puntí, Gaudí had picked up knowledge the trades of carpenter, blacksmith, potter and glazier.

According to Joan Bassegoda Nonell, a Barcelona architect who has studied in detail Gaudí's architectural development, "he found it equally interesting to design a door latch as a wardrobe or an entire building ... Throughout his career, Gaudí showed himself to be more a sculptor than an architect, and he was always happier making clay or plaster models than making plans or drawings."

But such a singular fashion of approaching the architect's trade could only be commissioned by clients who were also somewhat singular. And there was certainly no shortage of such individuals in the Barcelona of the time.

III

By now, Antoni Gaudí had been in Barcelona for ten years. The vibrant city attracted people from all around, and the newcomers, still lost in the anonymity of the metropolis, instinctively struck up relationships with other nomads or immigrants from their own place of origin. People who, if they had remained in their home towns of Reus, Igualada or Mataró would probably have exchanged no more than a 'Hello', if that, or —who knows?— would have been sworn enemies, suddenly became firm friends on running into each other in Barcelona.

The nostalgia of a childhood or landscape shared in medium-sized towns, the common roots of the local tribe, help to explain many things. And so, Antoni Gaudí suddenly came into contact with another native of Reus, a certain Salvador Pagés, who, moreover, was also a rather unusual character.

Pagés, who was twice Gaudí's age, was a self-made man and a fervent disciple of the progressionist movement then in vogue. According to someone who had known him personally, "Pagés had lived for some years in the United States and had returned from New York with a fortune. He had arrived in Catalonia with his son, whom he had named Lincoln by civil process." In the United States, Lincoln was a common surname, but it had been made charismatic by the country's first president, Abraham Lincoln (1809-1865). But as a Christian name it sounded eccentric to Catalan ears. It also demonstrated a revolutionary rejection of the age-old tradition of Christian Europe of christening children with the names of saints.

In Catalonia, giving a child a name not included in the list of Catholic saints, by means of a civil process without going through the religious ceremony of baptism, had only ever been possible during the ephemeral existence of the First Spanish Republic in 1873. Even so, few parents had made use of this short-lived right. Some followers of Tolstoy's style of anarchism named their daughters Armonia; Llibert was chosen as a boy's name by anarchists who idealised the figure of the freed slave. There were even a few parents who had given their children extravagant names drawn from poorly-digested readings: such was the case of a member of the Association of Free-Thinkers of Barcelona, who named his son Zoroastro in evident allusion to Zarathustra, the mythical prophet of pre-Christian Persia who was popularised by the book *Thus Spake Zarathustra* by the German philosopher F.W. Nietzsche, who ended his life in insanity in 1900. Not, perhaps, an auspicious sign. The poor son of the free-thinker died shortly after birth. The name Lincoln was, at least, easy on the ear.

IV

All we appear to know about Salvador Pagés is that he was born in Reus in 1833, that he was a weaver, "a worker with no education but a clear understanding" according to a newspaper of the time. At the age of 31 he is documented again in Reus, moving soon afterwards to Barcelona, where he became "one of the foremost leaders of the cooperativist mechanical weavers." What kind of fortune could he have made in the intervening ten or so years? We have no basis for making any conjecture.

What is clear is that at the age of 36 Pagés was the general manager of the cooperative La Obrera Mataronesa, established in the town of Mataró, with a population of 27,000, situated on the coast some 30 kilometres north of Barcelona, with which it was connected by what had been the first railway built in the Iberian Peninsula.

A local journalist described him as "our good friend Salvador Pagés, whom the workers must respect and venerate as a hero of work." Pagés was an enterprising man who had made his cooperative the first factory in the Peninsula to install electric lighting, whose sparks served as the triumphant announcement of the Progress which was to bring happiness to the human race.

Pagés wanted to build in Mataró a group of individual houses for workers on lands which were then allotments, and he had instilled his enthusiasm in both humble labourers and young 'classless' intellectuals such as Joaquim Maria Bartrina i d'Aixemus, another native of Reus. Bartrina, a young romantic suffering from tuberculosis, was inspired by the theories of Darwin, was a stylish writer and believed in a better future for mankind. Bartrina would be the ideal publicist for the planned workers' colony.

The ideal architect would be another compatriot from Reus: that red-headed young man with the penetrating gaze, Antoni Gaudí i Cornet.

CHAPTER 9

Utopia

I

Salvador Pagés, the wealthy admirer of Lincoln, was a mature, experienced man with great power of persuasion. And Gaudí, who was 25 and had a head full of ideas ready to be developed, allowed himself to be convinced by his fellow Reus native. If you don't believe in utopias when you're 25, when will you believe in them?

Some periods are more propitious than others for ideas about utopias. And the time of Gaudí's early adulthood certainly was propitious. When people travelled in horse-drawn coaches, in a sleepy little town in the heart of France, a certain Jules Verne was writing *De la terre a la lune*, a vision of astronauts from Earth walking on the surface of our pale satellite. Another Frenchman, Alphonse de Lamartine, who died in 1869, had left as his political testament this idea: "Utopia is reality brought forward".

There was also something Utopian in the way Gaudí had approached the project of the workers' colony in Mataró. Originating in Great Britain, industrial colonies had also begun to be built in Catalonia. Gaudí had never been to Britain, and so had never witnessed the wretched sight of the rows of workers' houses with naked façades, pressed one against the other via party walls, and standing virtually alongside the workplaces, whether the mines of South Wales or the cotton mills of Lancashire. There, the Industrial Revolution had turned Blake's 'green and pleasant land' into the Black Country of Dickensian times.

Apparently alien to social factors, to anything not originating in his own personal vision, Gaudí imagined an ideal housing estate: 30 detached houses surrounded by gardens, laid out in three rows near the sea, in such a way that they would all have sunlight in both the morning and afternoon and would be sheltered from the winds. Far removed from the stinking fumes of the chimneys of the city, each happy cooperative worker's house would have a plot of land of 200 m^2, partly occupied by the vegetable patch or garden. The house would have a ground floor and basement and would measure 12 by 9 metres. The façade would be topped by a triangular pediment similar to those of Greek and Roman temples. Lower down, between the two windows and the front door, there would be simple painted floral motifs.

Altogether, the workers' houses planned by Gaudí prefigured many of those which nowadays, over a century later, are only accessible to the tasteless *nouveaux riches* of the suburbs of Barcelona.

II

On 29th March 1878, Gaudí signed the construction plan of the first house of the idyllic development project. He was also commissioned other, lesser works of an industrial nature.

The cooperativists' enthusiasm led them to want their own banner or standard. The standards of Catalan corporations and civic groups were similar to those carried by Protestant associations in Northern Ireland, or by the Roman legions in Hollywood epics. The banner hung from a horizontal bar attached to a vertical metal pole, with a metal emblem fixed above it. Every self-respecting popular society in the 19th century had its own banner, whether it was a society, a guild, a choir, a scientific association, or a company. And so La Obrera Mataronesa had to have its own banner.

Designing banners would not seem to be a task one expects an architect to carry out: but Antoni Gaudí, who was clearly so good with his hands, so skilful in manual trades, so imaginative and original, was also commissioned to conceive and design the banner of the happy cooperative workers.

That Gaudí should be both willing and happy to do this job and, moreover, for little or no financial remuneration, would seem to indicate that he, too, was a convinced cooperativist, an innocent believer in the fraternal equality of men. But this is not the case.

III

A spirit as withdrawn, imaginative, original, teeming with ideas and selective of affinities as was Gaudí's could in no way be merely one more member of an association, whatever it might be. He might applaud the principles underlying the association and enjoy the company of its members: but it is difficult to imagine him forming a stable part of the collective organism. He might be a sympathiser of Utopian socialism, and indeed he was, as was, in one way another, everyone in the social circles of Mataró in which he was involved at that time.

The architect Bergós, who was Gaudí's assistant, left the testimony that his master "in his youth had been *infected* by the socialist movement which was starting up in England." But Gaudí's temperament and character were, without doubt, those of someone who flees in horror from the gregarious nature of the masses. If his relationship with the circle of Mataró continued for over a decade, it is because there was another reason, more private, more intimate.

CHAPTER 10

Uncle Anton

I

Gaudí's sister Rosa was the only surviving female member of the Gaudí-Cornet family following the death of the mother. She was the first child, and had always been rather delicate. She had married a poor musician who had fallen into bohemian ways and the perils of alcohol, and it is unclear whether he eventually died of drink or simply disappeared from the family scene.

A family's first child is inevitably burdened with the parents' greatest expectations and disappointments. And Rosa, complying faithfully with the designs of fate, died one day in 1879, at the age of only 35, leaving behind her an orphan girl of three, also named Rosa.

Excluding the collateral relatives, of what was strictly speaking the Gaudí-Cornet family there now only remained the father, Francesc, and the youngest child, Anton, who was 27.

The father was 66 years old but showed tremendous resistance against both illness and misfortune. He saw the withering of the branches of the family tree he had planted with Antònia Cornet. He watched the fruits fall to the ground one after the other to fertilise the World Below, while he, against all expectations and apparently against the laws of nature, survived them all.

The surviving son, Antoni, although he was now making a place for himself in the world, lacked the inner strength of his father. And he had not yet planted his own family tree.

With the death of his sister, Antoni became the protecting uncle of his little niece. But there is no evidence that his intimate vocation was that of becoming the clichéd, affectionate figure of the 'uncle who never married', who was present in many families. On the contrary, all of the evidence indicates that Antoni Gaudí was characterised by a virility that was alert, natural, and perhaps even as powerful as his father's, and that he wanted to marry — and wanted this more as the years passed.

A story entitled *La Calaverada* ('The Prank') by the Catalan poet Joan Maragall, who was a friend of Gaudí, is reputed to be based on real-life episodes from Gaudí's student days, when he felt a strong attraction for a girl he had met. The story dates from the early 1900's, when elegant society considered that sexual attraction was not a fitting theme to be discussed in print, or that at most it was a subject for novelists, who, after all, were hardly respectable individuals anyway.

It was a man from a subsequent generation, Carles Soldevila, a cultured writer who shone between the two World Wars, who found credible the supposed adventures of the young Gaudí. He said, "Is the protagonist of Maragall's story Gaudí, or at least an image of Gaudí? If he is, we have before us a new facet of this extraordinary man, and a very sympathetic facet at that."

In the middle years of the 20th century, descendants of collateral relatives of Gaudí also related imprecise stories of other girls who had attracted the young student but who had paid him little or no attention. All in all, the type of banal and habitual anecdotes that could be told about any relatively normal man. Scraps of stories which show no originality nor arouse any particular interest nor surprise.

II

Having become the protecting uncle of his niece, whom he called Rossita, Gaudí enrolled her in a nuns' school and did not limit himself to merely paying the corresponding fees. Despite his reputation of being gloomy and withdrawn, Uncle Anton, who now wore a think, pointed beard, must have felt for his niece that tenderness typical of unmarried uncles or aunts, particularly when the child is an orphan. Proof of this is that, having been invited one day by Salvador Pagés of Mataró to meet two daughters of the well-to-do and cultured Moreu family of the town, Gaudí appeared holding his niece by the hand.

The scene is related in his memoirs by Josep Maria Moreu, the younger brother of the two sisters, who was then 12 or 13. "One day, in the large dining-room of the house, we had as a guest a young architect from Reus called Gaudí ... He was accompanied by a niece, Rossita, of about my age ... Gaudí was fair-haired. His niece Rossita was somewhat darker, and perhaps rather plain, but to me she seemed very likeable ... Gaudí was very comfortable there ..."

The Moreus had a welcoming, single-storey house with a flower-filled garden. The French taste was evident. In one corner of the broad dining-room there was an Adolphe Lorch piano from Paris, and the room was redolent of family life. The warm presence of the women of the family was palpable, in great contrast to the chilly apartment that Gaudí shared with his old father.

Gaudí often visited the Moreu house and entered their circle of acquaintances. Time passed. Several years passed. The man who on finishing his studies displayed a thick head of hair now realised he was beginning to turn bald. And one day he made up his mind. He would continue to be Uncle Anton, but he would be Uncle Anton *with a wife.*

He plucked up determination and proposed marriage to the elder sister, Josefa Moreu..

CHAPTER 11

A love in Mataró

I

It is possible that when Gaudí made his proposal of marriage to Josefa Moreu, she was still involved in the lengthy process of annulling a first marriage with a certain Antoni Palau from Calella, a coastal town some 20 kilometres north of Mataró. It was said of Palau, as it was of Salvador Pagés, that he had made a fortune in the Americas. It is probable that the marriage had never been consummated, and that it had never been formalised in church, bearing in mind the Moreu family's known aversion to the clergy.

At any rate, Josefa, who was affectionately known as Pepeta, was younger than Gaudí and truly eye-catching. She was slim, with fine features and "hair of a reddish-gold colour, almost mahogany, and she had a rare beauty", in the words of her nephew Enric Moreu-Rey.

Her physical attractiveness was complemented with a dazzling personality which blended elegance of manners with extreme modernity of ideas and actions.

Josefa Moreu knew how to swim, and she swam at the beach, something which, in those days, even though bathing costumes reached the knees, made her something of a shameless hussy in the eyes of conservative society. She played the piano. She sang. She spoke French. She gave classes in the workers' cooperative. She read the Republican newspapers. She and her sister associated with social-

67

ists, anti-monarchists, free-thinkers, freemasons, advocates of the independence of Catalonia, naturalists, hygienists, homeopaths ... and spiritualists.

Nicolau Guanyabens, the Moreu family's doctor and close friend, had given Josefa a book by Allan Kardec, the apostle of spiritualism, to enlighten her in the then-new belief in the communication with the souls of the departed.

A vibrant young middle-class woman like this, "intellectual, with advanced and anti-clerical ideas", as her brother defined her, must surely have made a powerful impression on the timid Antoni Gaudí.

II

Since he had started to earn money, Gaudí wore finely-tailored suits and smoked long cigars. He had a solid rather strong build. He was of medium height, and his head resembled those of the busts of imperial Rome seen in the museums of Tarragona, Barcelona, Paris and elsewhere. His loss of hair was compensated by a thick but close-cropped beard which framed his regular, rounded features.

He knew a wealth of things about the most diverse matters and their causes, but on first meeting he would have been taken merely as an honest tinsmith dressed in his Sunday best rather than as a man of culture.

The refined city ways of dealing with women, of moving in society, of sitting, of folding a handkerchief or a napkin, all of these things were alien to the son and grandson of rural craftsmen. His manner was reserved and abrupt even with men; relating to women must have been even more difficult for him.

Gaudí was skilful with clay, plaster, stone, glass, wood, iron, brass, with the draughtsman's triangle and set-square, compass and pen, but he was clumsy when it came to picking up a knife and fork. He was not the type to check whether his trousers were creased, not to look in the mirror on entering a house to see if his parting was neat.

His poor mother, a faithful devotee of Our Lady of Mercy, whose icon presided over the entrance of the house in Reus, had brought him up in the age-old peasants' and craftsmen's fashion, and had taught him to pray and little else. Such hard-working folk rarely treated their children with much refinement. We cannot know whether Gaudí had lacked affection in his youth, or whether he felt that he had, but if so, it would surely have made it harder for him to show affection himself.

It was from homes such as Gaudí's that men of severe features and stern characters originated. We can see some of them in portraits hanging in dark Galleries of Illustrious Sons of towns in the deep heartland of Catalonia. And if a picture of Gaudí is ever to be hung, he must be painted with that same severity of sculpted stone.

"Although my sister Pepeta admired the artistic genius in Gaudí, she wasn't attracted to the man, who in reality took little care of his appearance," recalled Josep Maria Moreu in his memoirs. The result was what could have been foreseen by any man not enclosed within himself as Gaudí was. Josefa Moreu turned him down.

III

Any interest Gaudí may still have had in the Mataró circle was vanishing. Josefa Moreu was soon to display a sparkling engagement ring. The fiancé was a local timber merchant, Mr. Ignasi Caballol.

Moreover, La Obrera Mataronesa was going downhill. The directors of the cooperative had stipulated that the members could build a house on their own account, provided they followed the plans drawn up by Mr. Gaudí, covering all the costs of construction themselves. This, in effect, would make them the owners of the own houses. Fine. But when the cooperative had enough money, it would *oblige* the owners to sell their houses to it. The proud owners would become mere tenants!

Most of the members of the cooperative were honest people with little learning and few resources, but they were not lacking in common sense. The initiative failed, and this, together with the economic crisis, meant that only two of the planned houses were ever built. One of them was for the general manager, Salvador Pagés, himself.

In 1887 the cooperative went into liquidation. Gaudí had other, more powerful, clients waiting for him. But now, having being rejected by the young woman from Mataró, his soul would bear another scar.

CHAPTER 12

The café of exalted ecstasies

I

For Gaudí, deprivation was now a thing of the past. His commissions were increasing, and so were his fees. His circle of acquaintances was also growing.

Among the technicians working on the new buildings in Barcelona there was Eduard Fontseré i Mestre, who, apart from being an architect, was or had been the president of a secret society, the Masonic lodge Lealtad ('loyalty'). His brother Josep Fontseré was also an architect, and had had Gaudí as an assistant when the latter was still a student. The Fontserés originated from Vinyols, a small village near Riudoms, and so the three men were united in the knowledge of being of the same 'tribe'.

Gaudí coincided with the architect Camil Oliveras in the Catalanist Association of Scientific Excursions, a society which, among other things, worked to ensure that buildings and other works of historic interest were not destroyed with the urban reforms that were being carried out so hastily in Barcelona and other towns.

Oliveras had planned a monument dedicated to Bakunin, the Russian prince who had advocated the universal anarchist revolution. However, this idea would seem to have been little more than a snob's conceit with the aim of *épater les bourgeois*, shocking the middle class. After all, Oliveras was appointed architect of the Barcelona Provincial Council and worked for the Company of Jesus (the

Jesuits), for the Diocese of Barcelona, for a count and for a marquis.

More kaleidoscopic was Eudald Canibell i Masbernat. This native of Barcelona, with his sharp nose, pointed ears and sharp eyes, was an artist, painter, typographer, bibliographer and journalist. Not content with all of this, he had also been a founder member of the Catalanist Association of Scientific Excursions, of which Gaudí was an active member between the ages of 27 and 37.

A man of anarchist ideas, Canibell's pseudonym in his Masonic lodge was 'Bakunin'. He had been a leader of the Federation of Workers of the Spanish Region, when this could place a person in considerable danger. In the region of Jerez, Andalusia, and under the banner of the revolution, a criminal band called La Mano Negra (the 'Black Hand') had formed, and proceeded to kidnap, torture and murder without scruples. The government declared that they were protected by the Federation of Workers, and in order to mark out distances, the Federation published a communiqué stating that the Andalusian group was formed "not of workers but thieves and killers". As a result, La Mano Negra threatened Canibell and other Federation leaders with death. Some time later, Canibell was recorded as saying, "It's a good thing that Jerez is a long way from Barcelona!"

Canibell's friendship with Gaudí did not originate from these events, however, but from the feelings and ambitions they shared. Among these was an interest in artistic and scientific naturalism, which they regarded as a means of regenerating and modernising Catalan society.

II

When a person stands out above the rest and this becomes clear to the public, sooner or later they will have to face the envy and ill-will of the peevish souls that surround them.

It has been written that the architect Lluís Domènech i Muntaner, a contemporary of Gaudí, started the rumour that as a young man Gaudí had frequented an anti-clerical *tertulia* or discussion group which met at the Café Pelai, situated at the top of the Rambla in Barcelona. To those who knew Gaudí in person, this story was no surprise at all. Josep Pijoan, professor of art history at the University of Chicago and also a contemporary of Gaudí, said that the latter was "a man criss-crossed with contradictions to an indescribable degree", and that "his religious crisis lasted many years."

The Café Pelai was the obligatory meeting place for intellectuals and artists of the Catalan capital. But its common denominator was not anti-clericalism but Catalanism. The building no longer exists, but a vivid description of its atmosphere has been conserved thanks to the pen of the Russian Jewish writer Issac Iakovlevich Pavlovski, a nihilist who had lived in exile in France and Switzerland and spent a few months in Barcelona in 1884.

"I have travelled a great deal in my life," wrote Pavlovski, "but I have never come across people as sincere and pure of heart as in Catalonia, the poetic country of the troubadours ... From the Pyrenean countryman to the elegant, well-read capitalist gentleman of the city ... they all speak in Catalan and cannot abide Spanish ... The children do not understand Spanish before going to school. The simple people regard the Spanish as foreigners, much as our *mugik* [Russian peasant] regards the Turks or the Germans ... If a Catalan peasant has to appear before a court, he needs an interpreter, because the judges are often from other parts of Spain and do not understand Catalan."

Pavlovski adds that "Every working day at two o'clock in the afternoon, winter or summer, the Catalanists begin to arrive at the Café Pelai, where they gather around a table in a room overlooking both the Rambla and Carrer Pelai ... I still recall their agitated discussions, the hopes expressed by my Catalan friends, their exalted ecstasies and justified indignations. This café is a true institution in Catalonia, as if it were a parliament..."

The tireless — and perhaps explosive — engine boiling inside of Gaudí made him burn up periods of life quickly. And so, full of doubts and contradictions, he allowed himself to be led by a veteran architect, Joan Martorell i Montells.

A man of an extraordinarily good nature and great religious devotion, Martorell overlooked Gaudí's excesses and possibly understood him better than many others. At any event, Martorell, who was twenty years older, opened wide to him the doors which do not open for everyone, those of earthly glory, and even half-opened to him the doors to the beyond.

PART FOUR

CHAPTER 13

Fortunes from America

I

The patient, veteran architect Joan Martorell had had the young Gaudí as an assistant and had realised that he was a diamond in the rough. Martorell taught him to solve by means of geometry problems of the necessary equilibrium which buildings must maintain. This saved the use of complicated mathematical formulas, which were not Gaudí's strong point.

The master Martorell took his young assistant under his wing and then gave him wings of his own. He introduced him to the ideal client: Eusebi Güell, a heavyweight in the world of big business in Catalonia and Spain. The heir to a rapidly-accumulated fortune, Eusebi Güell i Bacigalupi, eight years older than Gaudí, was married to the imperious heiress to a fortune which was possibly even greater, and which certainly had darker origins.

She was Isabel López, the daughter of Antonio López López, the son of a poor family from the village of Comillas on the Cantabrian coast. López had emigrated to the then Spanish colony of Cuba at the age of 14. Twenty years later he returned to Spain with an incredible fortune. How had he made it? Largely though dealing in African slaves.

On returning to Spain, López settled in the Catalan capital, in the house of the Vidal Quadras family from Sitges, who had also made their fortune in the Americas. López founded companies and banks, bought mines, railways, estates ... and acquiescence, collaboration, collusion. And like the Machiavellian dukes of the Italian Renaissance, he had at his service an honest priest, Jacint Verdaguer, who would later become the great romantic poet of the Catalan language.

Comillas, a dreary mining village, became his own private estate, where he built ostentatious mansions and monuments. Moved partly by vanity and partly by the desire to forget his ignominious colonial past, López also financed a hospital in his native village, and, in particular, a building dedicated to the Pontifical Seminary, an institution dedicated to young men preparing for the Roman Catholic priesthood.

To be sure, López's 'good works' in Comillas were not precisely what the Gospels meant. But, as the ancient Romans said, *Peculia non oliet* —money has no smell. This must also have been the idea of the Spanish King Alfonso XII, of the French Bourbon dynasty, when in 1878 he granted López the title of Marquis of Comillas.

If ever there was a marriage of convenience to rival those of the sons and daughters of royalty, it was the union between Eusebi Güell and Isabel López. The inheritance of the movable and immovable properties, industrial and financial assets, of both families condemned Eusebi Güell to be a shark of the business world.

But the heir had none of the prototypical characteristics of the predators of the money jungle. His tastes inclined towards drawing, watercolour painting, architecture, literature, the study of Romance languages — primarily Catalan and French — and the amateur cultivation of the sciences. And all of this was quite new in the Güell family, as Eusebi was the son of a self-made man who had had no time in life for such delicacies.

The Güell family were from Torredembarra, a village of barefoot fishermen, peasants and shepherds in the Camp de Tarragona which exported liquors to the Americas. Eusebi Güell's paternal grandfather had sought his fortune in this business in the Caribbean colony of Santo Domingo, but had died ruined. Then his son, Joan Güell, tried his luck, emigrating to Cuba at the age of 18. He came to practically monopolise the liquor market in Havana, and he returned to Catalonia seventeen years later, in 1835, a wealthy man.

No less than Antonio López López, Joan Güell had the mettle of men determined to climb the social ladder two steps at a time. First he bought a factory, then another, and another; he acquired a seat as a Municipal Councillor for Barcelona, a Member of Parliament and a Senator; all that remained was to have his own architect, and for this position he chose his devoted Joan Martorell, whose brother Àngel was also on the payroll, as the manager of Güell's most important factory.

On his father's death, Eusebi Güell also wanted to have his own architect. Joan Martorell advised him to pick Antoni Gaudí. Witnesses of the time agree that patron and architect struck up a good relationship. But Mr. Eusebi Güell did not yet know who he was really coming up against.

III

The first commission, or one of the first, that Eusebi Güell gave Gaudí was to design a hunting pavilion on a property he had on the coast near Barcelona. He soon began to talk of remodelling the mansion where he lived just off the Rambla of Barcelona, and also of reforming an estate with stables and a large garden in the green outskirts of the city, which he had inherited from his father.

The self-esteem of the very wealthy demands suitable surroundings to lend them a certain pedigree. The estate was situated halfway up a hill in the old municipal district of Sarrià, which was annexed by the city of Barcelona later in the 20th century. It was surrounded by fields where shepherds and goatherds still took their flocks to graze. But at the top of the rise there stood the medieval Clarissine convent of Santa Maria de Pedralbes, an emblem of the times of the knights and an honourable refuge of princesses and respectable young ladies fleeing from the perversities of the world.

Inside the grounds of the convent, a sumptuous alabaster tomb guarded the remains of its founder, Elisenda de Montcada, Queen of Catalonia and Aragón, who died there in 1364. Beneath the cold flagstones there lay the remains of the nuns, most of them daughters of the Catalan nobility of the time when Catalonia, a sovereign nation entirely independent of Castile and France, was lord and master of the Mediterranean.

It was in this spot, within the sound of the prayer bells, that Eusebi Güell would cultivate his own mythological garden. All Gaudí had to do was to create the stage setting.

IV

Even before finishing the works on the Güell Estate in Pedralbes, Gaudí embarked on many other projects. In those days his creative imagination overflowed. He was in demand from other bourgeois patrons, and still had relations with the Mataró circle. He often applied similar solutions to different commissions, which meant that his own recognisable style was taking shape.

The American professor George R. Collins observed: "Gaudí's style of architecture went through several phases. On emergence from the Provincial School of Architecture in Barcelona in 1878, he practised a rather florid Victorianism that had been evident in his school projects, but he quickly developed a manner of composing by means of unprecedented juxtapositions of geometric masses, the surfaces of which were highly animated with patterned brick or stone, gay ceramic tiles, and floral or reptilian metal-work. The general effect, although not the details, is Moorish, or *mudéjar*, as Spain's special mixture of Muslim and Christian design is called. Examples are the Casa Vicens (1878-80) ... and the Güell Estate and Güell Palace of the later 1880's... Next, Gaudí experimented with the dynamic possibilities of historic styles, Gothic and Baroque..."

V

In the middle of this period, Joan Martorell had to solve a delicate matter. The temple that had been imagined some time before by Friar Manyanet, the founder of the insti-tutes of the Children of the Holy Family, had had its first stone laid in 1882. The stubborn bookseller with clair-voyant's eyes, old Mr. Josep Maria Bocabella, had succeeded in collecting the money needed to start turning the project into reality. The works had been commissioned to the architect Francisco de Paula del Villar, a decent old chap from Murcia in the south-west of the Peninsula who worked for the Diocese of Barcelona and who had been one of Gaudí's professors.

In professional terms Villar was known to be something of a mediocrity, and soon after the plans were finalised and the construction of the crypt began, for one reason or another the first discrepancies arose. Villar wanted to arrange the columns of the crypt in one way, and the architectural advisor of Bocabella the promoter, who was none other than Joan Martorell, wanted them a different way. They argued, and Villar resigned.

At that point it occurred to Martorell that Antoni Gaudí, who had once helped him to build a convent, could take over the works for the new Temple of the Holy Family. After all, it was a fairly routine task. The plans were already drawn up. There was just one inconvenience. Old Mr. Bocabella and the Josephine Association were staunch Apostolic Roman Catholics. And Gaudí was not exactly a dedicated churchgoer.

CHAPTER 14

Premonition, or visions of another world

I

Bocabella and Gaudí knew little or nothing about each other. The young architect must have heard of the visionary bookseller who had collected enough donations to build a new temple in Barcelona. But it is unlikely that Bocabella, who was now close to 70, would have known anything of the existence of Martorell's young assistant, let alone of his skills or beliefs. However, Bocabella had an unshakeable faith in Martorell, so when the latter proposed that Gaudí should take charge of the continuation of the recently-initiated works on the Sagrada Família, Bocabella raised no objection. After all, if the Josephine Association didn't like the new architect's way of doing things, they would look for another, as simple as that.

First impressions are lasting impressions. At first sight, Gaudí was distinguished from the majority by his fair hair. This alone, obviously, meant nothing. But this whim of nature was accompanied by another characteristic, also relatively unusual in the southern regions of Catalonia: he had blue eyes. Blue eyes! Just as one of Bocabella's relatives had predicted!

Pious Aunt Joaquima had had a revelation, a divine inspiration, according to the *josefins* —or perhaps a premonition, as the rationalists would prefer to believe, since premonitions are proven phenomena. And according to this revelation or premonition— which occurred shortly before the interview between Bocabella and Gaudí in

Martorell's office —"the architect of the Temple of the Holy Family would have blue eyes". What importance did this detail have?

II

It is well known that each of the primary colours causes a different psychological reaction. To the human eye, blue produces a more pleasant reaction than black. In communities with a predominance of dark eyes, blue eyes stand out. And it is a popular tradition to admire blue eyes and to believe that they indicate goodness of character.

It is not surprising, then, that this belief should penetrate the religious imagination of simple folk, and that in one way or another it should survive to this day in Catalonia. In the various towns where Christ's Passion is re-enacted by local amateur actors, it is still an axiom that the actor playing St. Joseph should have blue eyes. And this idea was stronger still in the 19th century, when the de-Christianising of society was just beginning.

III

The few photographs of Gaudí which have survived are in black and white, and therefore it is impossible to discern the colour of his eyes. We can, however, see a magnetic gaze. The priest Llorenç Riber, a contemporary of the architect, went further, referring to "those eyes of his ... that were at the same time enchanting and frightening".

Descriptions of people are very subjective. They often mix objective details confirmed by other people with the more or less flowery imagination of the writer. At any event, it is significant that a number of Gaudí's contemporaries should leave written testimony of Gaudí's eyes and the look emanating from them.

The journalist Jaume Bofill wrote: "Gaudí looked his listeners in the face and held them *with the light in his eyes* and in his words". Another revealing testimony was left by Miquel Farrà, a librarian of the University of Barcelona in the early decades of the 20th century, who was considerably younger than Gaudí and had therefore known him only as an old man, but closely, and said of him, "I have never seen in anyone's look so much joyous light and gentle humility combined with such a hard, penetrating gleam. His eyes could sear through vanity and empty pomposity like bolts of lightning, but caress with adoring indulgence everything pure and beautiful in this world and the visions of the other."

CHAPTER 15

Extravagances

I

"This looks like a barber's shop!" cried the imperious Mrs. López in horror. She was the mistress of the new house that Gaudí was building for her husband, Eusebi Güell, in the Carrer Nou de la Rambla in Barcelona. It is easy to suppose that the artistic tastes of the ex-slaver Antonio López López were execrable. But it is no less evident that Gaudí's fervid architectural incontinence also transgressed the normal limits.

The good lady did not approve of the shape of the windowed gallery that was being added to the façade of the house. But there was little she could do about it, because her husband accepted without a murmur each of Gaudí's successive fantasies.

Nevertheless, what is most surprising to any modern-day mind endowed with a modicum of common sense is not so much the teeming imagination of the architect but the possibility that any family could ever have seriously considered living in one of Gaudí's uncomfortable, discordant houses.

The central sitting-room of what was supposed to be the home of the Güell-López family was no less than a representation of the cosmos! Looming over it and entirely dominating the space was a celestial dome, the technical solution of which has been described by the present-day architect Joan Bassegoda, without a trace of irony, as "a solution similar to that of the dome of St. Paul's Cathedral in London."

The spectacular and capricious nature of the house, now called the Palau Güell or Güell Mansion, distantly recalls the mansion of the pitiful Gloria Swanson in the film *Sunset Boulevard*.

Eusebi Güell and Isabel López did not live many years in the house. Its theatrical vocation was fully realised years later when it was converted into the Theatre Museum of the Catalan capital.

And the question is, how is it possible that Gaudí's clients allowed him so much room for individual manoeuvre?

II

Until the second half of the 20th century, the construction of houses was overseen by anonymous builders or masons. The cities of Europe conserve innumerable examples of solid, useful, pleasing buildings raised over the generations by honest craftsmen, many of whose names go unrecorded by history.

But the inexorable increase in complexity in science, in technology and in daily life itself demands that the designers of buildings have high-level studies which are no longer accessible to all. One result of this process was the creation in 1871 of the School of Architecture of Barcelona.

A new individualism was imposing itself. Many painters were demanding to be recognised as *artists*, as individuals touched by a special gift, and refused to work to commission and to be regarded as mere anonymous artisans or tradesmen. Similarly, the recently-qualified architects wanted to set themselves apart from the tradesmen and to be considered part of group of a superior status.

And the time was ripe. The self-made men returning from the Americas and the new bourgeois families of the rapidly-expanding city of Barcelona were anxious to demonstrate that they had succeeded in life. And the most visible manner of satisfying this human weakness was to erect an ostentatious house that was very different from the neighbours'. Consequently, the mason or architect had to be an individual with imagination, not necessarily with good taste.

In these circumstances, Gaudí was clearly the right man in the right place at the right time. From his brain spouted a fountain of imagination as dense and mysterious as any jungle, and he had the audacity of the true eccentric.

III

As surprising as Gaudí's works themselves was the extremely personal manner in which he carried out the commissions of his successive clients and the relationships he had with them.

For Mr. Manuel Vicens, a Catalan pottery manufacturer, he built a house in Gràcia which is entered by a door which seems to be that of the palace of an oriental sultan. The interior of the Vicens House displays many other details of Gaudí's graceful adaptation of the then fashionable 'Islamic' style.

The unsuspecting Eusebi Güell intended his estate near Pedralbes to be a welcoming haven of peace. Incomprehensibly, Gaudí made the broad main entrance gate in the form of a vast wrought-iron dragon whose ferocious, gaping mouth threatened to swallow the visitor whole!

The imprint of Gaudí's personal style remained engraved in stone even in those projects which did not meet with their foreseen ends.

In 1887, Monsenyor Joan Grau had just been appointed Bishop of Astorga, in the province of León in Castile, where the old episcopal palace had recently been destroyed by a fire. The bishop, yet another native of Reus, chose Gaudí as the architect for a new building, and the two men struck up an excellent working relationship. But the authorities in Madrid raised numerous objections, the Castilian clergy did all they could to prevent the project of 'the Catalans' from taking shape, and after Bishop Grau died in 1893, the temperamental Gaudí abandoned the work in disgust. The building was completed, to no-one's satisfaction, in 1907. Even so, Gaudí managed to leave his unmistakable mark on it. Nowadays, seen from a distance, the palace looks like some Gothic fortress on the Rhine, which neither Gaudí, Grau nor the local clergy intended. It has never been in-habited by the bishops, and is now known as the Gaudí Palace and serves as an exhibition hall.

IV

Some of the stories told about Gaudí speak of his bad luck, understood not in the vulgar sense of the term as meaning-less chance events, but of the ill fortune spoken of by the occult sciences and superstitious people. One such case is the Calvet House, situated at number 48 of Carrer Casp in Barcelona.

Pere Màrtir Calvet was an industrialist from Vilassar de Mar, between Barcelona and Mataró, who had made a fortune in the textile trade. He wanted Gaudí to be the designer of the house that he intended to build in the very heart of business and society life, the centre of the capital.

Neither the owner nor the architect spared any expense. To begin with, the iron handrails of the house were edged with fine gold. According to the researcher Jordi Elias, "circumstance had brought together two equally fanciful men: the manufacturer, extravagant and carefree, and the architect, oblivious to practical sense, averse to budgets and moderation." However, despite this mutual empathy, the client had to put his foot down on one notable occasion.

The architect was proposing to occupy the doorway with nothing less than a drawbridge, like that of a medieval castle! Needless to say, the bridge was never built.

The house was completed in 1900 and won the City Council's first-ever prize for new buildings, but only on a divided vote. The most interesting detail of its façade is the number of wild mushroom designs adorning the wrought-iron balcony rails and stonework, reflecting the fact that Calvet was something of an expert in this ancestral and occasionally dangerous Catalan delicacy.

But the imaginative Mr. Calvet was not to enjoy his 'mushroom house' for very long. He fell into financial ruin and had to sell the house, in 1927, to a certain Joan Boyer. Calvet went from owning the house to being a tenant in it. He paid his last rent bills with the few belongings and pieces of furniture remaining to him. It is said that he died abandoned and penniless.

Another story of misfortune is the following. Having just completed a Gothic-style house named Bellesguard (after the mansion of the last King of Catalonia, which had stood nearby) in the Collserola hills above Barcelona, Gaudí was asked by the owner to place a lightning conductor at the top of its exaggeratedly tall and slender spire. Gaudí reputedly replied that this was not necessary, since lightning had never fallen in the area and it was unwise to 'tempt fate'. The owner insisted, and the lightning rod was installed. A few days later, an infernal storm broke out ... and the house was struck by lightning.

V

In Barcelona's elegant central boulevard of Passeig de Gràcia, the industrialist Josep Batlló owned a conventional block of flats, which he commissioned Gaudí to reform and modernise. If his intention was to attract attention, Batlló certainly never had reason to complain.

At first sight, the Batlló House looks like an elves' mansion from the world of Tolkien. Seeking an explanation for the building's extraordinary appearance, the people of Barcelona gave it, among others, the name of 'the house of bones', because the columns of the lower part of the façade seemed to resemble the tibias, fibulas, vertebrae, collarbones and skull of the human body.

The whole building was extremely unusual, but Batlló continued to pay for every one of the costly inventions imposed by the architect, who paid no attention to the practical suggestions occasionally made to him by the owners.

Josep Batlló had a weak character, but his wife was one of the Godó family, who were not inclined to stand for any nonsense. The family originated from the inland town of Igualada, which they had eventually come to dominate. Joan Godó, who had been the mayor at the end of the 19th century, was known as 'el morrut' for his glowering expression. Another branch of the family, which was later to found Barcelona's illustrious liberal newspaper *La Vanguardia*, settled for a time in Bilbao, where Joan Batlló's future wife was born.

Although she came from an eminent Catalan family, had married a Catalan and lived in the Catalan capital, Batlló's wife spoke only Castilian, following the example of the high-level bourgeoisie related to the ruling families in Madrid. Gaudí, in contrast, invariably expressed himself in Catalan. The hatred between the architect and his client's wife was mutual and intense. This, added to Gaudí's oblivious heedlessness, meant that things had to explode sooner or later. We do not know the details, but the outcome has been related in these terms: "With the house still unfinished, Gaudí was simply dismissed."

VI

Just three minutes' walk from Can Batlló, on the other side of Passeig de Gràcia, another Barcelona industrialist, Pere

Milà i Camps, had a discreet villa with a garden, on a property which was once occupied by a chapel dedicated to the Mare de Déu del Roser (Our Lady of the Rose-tree).

Milà was the son of a business partner of the Godó clan, and he felt obliged to undertake the same ostentatious building initiatives. But perhaps he would never have dared to entrust his plans to Gaudí if it had not been for the influence of his wife, Roser Segimon, a beautiful and somewhat extravagant woman from, once again, Reus.

Roser Segimon had married Pere Milà after losing her first husband, Josep Guardiola, a trader from a village near Riudoms. Guardiola had made a fortune in Guatemala, and among other things he was a shareholder in the Panama Canal Company. This made him apparently just one more of so many Catalans who had successfully 'done the Americas'. But one thing set him far apart from the rest: one of those eccentricities with which the Catalans occasionally leave the world dumbfounded. In 1895, Guardiola published, in Paris, the grammar of a language which he had invented entirely by himself, and which no-one has ever attempted to understand. The title of the work was *Gramatica uti nove prata kiamso orba*...

With this background, and with the fortune inherited from Guardiola, Roser Segimon, already touched by extravagance and now married to Milà, commissioned the construction of one of the most ignominious buildings in Barcelona, the Monumental bullring.

Subsequently, she and her husband completed the circle of extravagances by commissioning Gaudí to build a large apartment block on the plot occupied by their villa and garden. As the new Casa Milà gradually arose from the ground, it began to take on jagged, wave-like forms that made it look more like a cliff face in the Rocky Mountains than a human construction. Small wonder that the locals soon began to call it 'La Pedrera', 'the quarry'.

It is said that the French statesman Georges Clemenceau saw the building during a short stay in

Barcelona, and swore that he had "no intention of returning to a city that could allow such a monstrosity to be built!"

Gaudí's idea was to crown the building with a colossal image of the Virgin Mary. The owners objected. The architect insisted. Had the property not been for centuries the home of the chapel of the Virgin? (And, precisely, the Virgin of the *Roser*?) —Then she must have her place in the house, and that could only be the most prominent place of all. Finally, the architect had reluctantly to submit. The image of the Virgin was not installed.

But this was not the only controversy. The final one occurred with the presentation of the bill. The owners refused to pay the amount Gaudí stated as his fees. Gaudí took the matter to the courts. The judges ruled in his favour. Pere Milà and Roser Segimon had to mortgage the building to pay the architect. Then, with his honour satisfied, Gaudí donated the whole amount to a convent.

The fact was that by now Gaudí was no longer working for money. He was heartily sick of serving the bourgeoisie, and the only goal he seemed to have any more was to continue with the works on the Temple of the Holy Family, which he had started so many years earlier.

With each passing year he appeared less interested in worldly matters. Jaume Bofill, a contemporary journalist who was inclined to irony and not at all enthusiastic about Gaudí's art, would later say, "Gaudí had been a perfectly respectable man of his time. The elegant, well-mannered gentleman who, some days, on arriving at the Sagrada Família, would not even get down from the carriage to give his instructions, gradually became won over by piety and drawn into the extremely austere life of a lay brother in a monastery."

As the art historian Manuel Trens said, "God is the only master with whom Gaudí finished on good terms."

CHAPTER 16

Goodbye, father!

I

"A madman who could allow himself mistakes, because he was dearly loved by the muses." This was what the Italian professor of art history Roberto Pane said of Gaudí. In Chicago, a collaborator of the architect Louis Henry Sullivan, whose designs of skyscrapers consisted of unremittingly straight lines, saw some photographs of the Sagrada Família under construction and exclaimed, "The author of this work is either a madman or a genius!"

Needless to say, true madmen are incapable of building cathedrals or temples like the Sagrada Família. But it is true that Gaudí's sometimes bizarre lines reveal a peculiar mind. A chronic arthritic illness, a tortured psychology and a series of depressions were, without doubt, elements present in Gaudí's life, and they clearly had some influence on his artistic expression.

II

At the age of 42, during the Lent of 1894, Gaudí made a fast so long and so extreme that he lost strength to an alarming extent. It was normal during Lent, the period of forty days before the Christian celebration of Easter, for Catholic families to practise some degree of fasting and abstinence, that is, to stop eating certain foods or to eat less of them. But Gaudí's fast, so exaggerated, and probably accompanied by a bout of depression, alarmed his father and his niece, who lived with him.

The family appealed to the technicians who were working on the Sagrada Família, asking them to visit Gaudí and persuade him to eat. They were unable to do anything, and in desperation the family appealed for help to a priest they knew, Josep Torras i Bages. Torras was an extremely short-sighted man, but strong and severe, and endowed, in the words of one writer, with a sonorous voice and the gift of finding the right word. His presence inspired respect.

Torras hurried to the house of the architect, and with the latter apparently on the threshold of the other world, he succeeded in persuading Gaudí to put an end to the sacrifice. And at that moment, while still recovering from his journey through the anterooms of death, Gaudí sat down at his desk, picked up a pencil and paper, and drew the first façade of the Temple of the Holy Family and a general sketch of the whole building.

III

One person who still took pleasure in living was the architect's father. The old coppersmith from Riudoms was a great walker, rivalled by few men of his age. His walks, his solid health and the naturalist habits recommended by the German priest Sebastian Kneipp, whose fame had by then reached Catalonia, had helped Francesc Gaudí to reach the grand old age of 91 and still be perfectly capable of smoking two or three *caliquenyo* cigars and walking, unaided, up and down the stairs to his fourth-floor flat in Carrer de la Diputació.

He had been a widower for almost thirty years. Of his five children, four were now dead. It seemed that all of the vital energies that had been lacking in the rest of the Gaudí-Cornet family were concentrated in him. He was

1. The dragon of the Parc Güell (Barcelona).

2. View of the Parc Güell.

3. Benches of the Parc Güell with fragments of ceramic tiles.

4. Building in the form of a Doric temple in the Parc Güell.

5. Doric-style colonnade of the Parc Güell.

6. Door of Casa Vicens (Barcelona).

7. Interior of Casa Vicens.

8. Casa Calvet, in Carrer de Casp (Barcelona).

9. Detail of the upper part of the façade of Casa Calvet.

10. Wrought-iron beetle decorating the door-knocker of Casa Calvet.

11. The reliefs of Casa Calvet include a large number of mushrooms.

12. Tower of Bellesguard (Barcelona).

13. Interior of the Bellesguard tower (private house).

14. Towers of the Sagrada Família (Barcelona).

15. Eastern façade of the Sagrada Família.

16. Anagram of Jesus Christ on the eastern façade of the Sagrada Família.

17. Every part of the Sagrada Família is replete with Catholic symbols

18. The eastern façade, dedicated to the Nativity of Christ, expresses the joy of living.

19. The figures on the Nativity façade are by the sculptor Matamala.

20. The stone cypress represented between the towers is a symbol of incorruptibility.

21. Fantastical decoration crowning the steeples of the Sagrada Família.

22.   Forest of columns in the Sagrada Família.

23. Wrought-iron dragon on the gate of the Finca Güell, in Avinguda de Pedralbes (Barcelona).

24. Parabolic roof of the Teresian Sisters' School in Carrer Ganduxer, Barcelona.

25. Casa Batlló, in Passeig de Gràcia (Barcelona).

26. The nocturnal illumination gives Casa Batlló a phantasmagorical appearance.

27. Window of Casa Batlló.

28. Casa Batlló: the four-armed cross in the foreground contrasts with the undulating roof (background) which simulates the scales of a dragon.

29. Detail of the undulating chimneys on the roofs of Casa Batlló.

30. Façade of «La Pedrera».

31. Chimneys of «La Pedrera».

32. A room in «La Pedrera».

33. Corridor of «La Pedrera».

34. Crypt of the Colònia Güell (Santa Coloma de Cervelló).

35. Interiors of the crypt of the unfinished church of the Colònia Güell.

broad-shouldered, of medium height, with a powerful head and regular features. He looked at people and things with a concentrated, scrutinising gaze like that of his son the architect. He was a man of few words, and when he did speak it was not about theories or abstract matters but about the land, the borders of the vineyards, the water, the streams running down from the mountains, the heat and the cold, the air and the winds.

In order for his father to live more peacefully, away from the traffic and bustle of the city, Antoni Gaudí bought a small house, built by another architect, in the grounds of the Parc Güell, an unfinished residential project promoted by Gaudí's patron Eusebi Güell, situated on the slopes of the Collserola hills on the northern edge of Barcelona.

So the father, the son and the niece Rossita, the orphan who had lived with them since she was small, moved to the hills. Gaudí's father had lived long enough to see how the fantastic shapes generated by the imagination of his only surviving son became materialised in stone. And how the stones were placed one on top of another and the spires of the Temple rose into the air like the cypress trees of the old cemetery in Riudoms, the cypress trees which are the symbols of eternity.

Now he could take his leave peacefully and say farewell to everything. Francesc Gaudí i Serra, the old coppersmith from Riudoms, the widower of Antònia Cornet, passed away on 29th October 1906, at 93 years of age.

The father's death had long been expected. But a son cannot imagine the blow it will mean for him until he collapses at the foot of the coffin. For Antoni Gaudí, whose 54 years had been lived almost constantly by his father's side, it was also the death of his most faithful companion in sorrows and fatigues.

IV

Following the death of his father, Gaudí immersed himself in the project of what was to be the church of the Güell Colony in Santa Coloma de Cervelló, a short distance from Barcelona. The first stone was laid in 1908, but only the crypt was ever built. It is probably the most ingenious of all of the architect's works, but it was to remain incomplete.

Ominous winds were blowing for the churches, and particularly for the Catalan churches.

CHAPTER 17

The day of the Beast, or the Tragic Week

I

July 26th 1909. The Day of the Beast. Great columns of smoke rose up and darkened the sun and the air. Barcelona shook with fear and hatred. From the rooftops, the smoke could be seen billowing from the towers of the churches.

What had started as a spontaneous revolt against the appalling working conditions and against the mobilisation of conscripts by the Spanish government for its colonial war in Morocco had turned unexpectedly into a religious persecution.

A week later, on 1st August, the toll was counted: eighty religious buildings pillaged and burned, three priests murdered, and the dead bodies of numerous nuns snatched from their graves and scattered in the streets. The rotting, mummified bodies of the nuns had been paraded through the city in scenes of brutal horror that even the mind of Hieronymus Bosch, the medieval Dutch painter of hellish delirium, could barely have imagined.

II

There was desperation among the working classes. In moments of crisis, the employers would declare a lock-out and condemn the workers to poverty. There were not many bosses like Eusebi Güell, who was generous to the employees of his Workers' Colony in Santa Coloma de Cervelló. Many employers — some of whom had come up from the mud themselves — said that "bread and onion is enough for the workers."

There was desperation and ignorance.

When Pope Leo XIII "rose up in a kind of holy rage against the abuses of the rich" with the publication of his encyclical *Rerum novarum*, the Spanish bishops silenced it. In Catalonia, the only one who had the courage to disseminate the text was Josep Morgades, the Bishop of Vic. (In Mexico, the fear of provoking the wrath of the wealthy was even stronger; the Bishop of San Luís de Potosí placed the document under lock and key in his cellar.)

There was desperation, ignorance and credulity.

The demagogy of the followers of Bakunin had heated up the ashes of the latent anti-clericalism of the proletariat of the cities, who had replaced the superstitious credulity of their rural ancestors with a credulity towards the incendiary urban agitators.

There was desperation, ignorance, credulity and manipulation.

Catalonia was witnessing at that time a re-emergence of the desire to recover its ancient national liberties, which had been crushed by the military power of Castile, which monopolised the central government in Madrid.

Henry Havelock Ellis, the English essayist, physician and psychologist, had perceptively observed in 1908 that "the Catalans are a robust and vigorous people who, since ancient times, have settled themselves firmly astride the eastern end of the Pyrenees, because it is easy to recognise the Catalan characteristics of the Roussillon. The Catalans are not French. Neither are they completely Spanish, even though they have mixed Spanish and French characteristics. Their irrepressible energy has enabled them to conserve a high degree of independence."

The desire to recover the ancient liberties was widespread in Europe.

Old Ireland, suffocated by England, was demanding Home Rule. Cyprus, with its indigenous Greek population, was asking the world for help in throwing off the military boot of Turkish occupation. Norway had gained its independence from Sweden as recently as 1905.

In the case of Catalonia, any internal conflict which could be aggravated, exploited and channelled towards chaos would provide an excellent excuse for the central government to justify sending in the army and penning the Catalans inside their cities. The Spanish State had suffered the traumatic loss of its colonies in Cuba and the Philippines in 1898, and it could not afford to lose both Morocco and Catalonia, too.

The Madrid government already had an effective *agent provocateur* in Catalonia: Alejandro Lerroux García, the son and brother of Andalusian military men, a frustrated aspirant to the Military Academy in Toledo, a self-proclaimed journalist who was a master of the language of the tavern. There is documentary proof that Lerroux was paid 1,000 pesetas per month — a fortune in those days — from the reserve funds of the Spanish Ministry of the Interior.

Lerroux, who had gained followers among the workers of Barcelona, not only Spanish immigrants but also some native Catalans, had written, "Workers! Lift up the veils of the novices and make them mothers! ... Do not stop before the graves nor before the altars ... destroy the temples!" And many of the city's churches were destroyed, but not Gaudí's temple.

III

The Tragic Week had a very profound impact on Catalan society. About the impact it had on the spirit, by then so religious, of Antoni Gaudí, we can only make suppositions. The fact is that six or seven months later he suffered a depression combined with anaemia. He had dizzy spells and could not stand up straight.

His friend Torras i Bages, who was now the Bishop of Vic, asked the local Jesuit priest Ignasi Casanovas to take care of the sick man. Father Casanovas, a respected and knowledgeable man, secured hospitality for Gaudí for a few weeks at the country house of Concepció Vila, the widow of Josep Rocafiguera, where the architect would find rest, distraction and nourishment. But after only a few days, Concepció Vila realised that it was much harder to deal with the sick man than she had thought. Perhaps a man would know better how to handle him?

She went to see a relative, Joaquim Vilaplana, an eminent apothecary of the city and patron of the arts. She said, "We don't what to with him. He hardly talks, he seems very sad ... He's got no appetite, we don't know what to serve him. I was thinking that you could help us out of the predicament. What will Father Casanovas say if Mr. Gaudí doesn't show some improvement?"

PART FIVE

CHAPTER 18

Death stalks the Parc Güell

I

At night, the spectre of death stalked the Parc Güell. Gaudí's health had improved a little with his few weeks' stay at Can Rocafiguera in Vic and with the walks he had taken in its surroundings. He had improved a little, but not much. On returning to Barcelona, to his new home in the Parc Güell, he again found himself face to face with his real self: a beaten man, tired of the world.

Both Gaudí and his niece Rossita suffered from the ghostly silence of the house, which reflected the absence of the warmth of a family. The sense of solitude had become even deeper since the death of Gaudí's father. Exhausted as he was, and preoccupied with the works of the Sagrada Família, it was often he who had to attend to the young woman.

Rossita had been an orphan since the age of three. At first she had been a lonely boarder at a convent school. Then she had become sickly like her mother, and probably bore the consequences of her father's alcoholism. She was prone to tuberculosis and heart disease, and possibly also to nervous crises. It was rumoured that she secretly used to drink 'Aigua del Carme', an alcohol-based drink made by the Carmelite nuns, which most families kept in the parlour as a remedy for fainting fits.

She sorely missed her grandfather, with whom she had gone out walking for so many years, and she must often have thought about how lonely she would be when Uncle Anton was no longer there.

It was fortunate that Gaudí could still count on the friendship of Pere Santaló, a doctor who always seemed to have everything under control, who often kept Gaudí company and took care of his health.

II

A good hiker and a good smoker, Dr. Santaló was also originally from the Camp de Tarragona, and he and Gaudí understood each other well. They each knew where the other had come from, and they had no need for social play-acting. Santaló could call Gaudí by the affectionate form of his first name, Anton.

But Rossita's health was failing and Uncle Anton was also worsening, and his mind was becoming absorbed by biblical images of the Temple. He had already finished the plan of the façade of the Birth of Jesus, facing east. But now he was thinking about how to draw the western façade, that of the Passion and Death.

He spent a lot of time thinking about death, and this was when he caught the Maltese fever, an infectious disease which, among other things, could cause arthritis or greatly aggravate it. The first thing the doctors recommended for this fever was a change of air. And so, leaving his niece in the company of a nun, a severely weakened Gaudí was taken by Santaló to a hotel in Puigcerdà, in the Catalan Pyrenees.

"You'll see, Mr. Gaudí, how you'll soon get well here," the hotel staff assured him.

III

By early June the sick man, who had little interest in getting well, felt even more ill than in Barcelona. So ill that

106

he thought his time had come. He decided to make his will. On 9th June 1911, he dictated his last wishes to the notary public of Puigcerdà Ramon Cantó.

On hearing via Dr. Santaló of Gaudí's state, people from other towns, mostly simple people, began to send packets of food and home-made remedies to Puigcerdà in the hope of helping him to recover.

Meanwhile, Mr. Antoni Gaudí, the famous designer of grand houses and mansions, the architect who had never once stopped to make even a modest sketch of what would be his own house, planned by himself, was already looking beyond the grave.

The traveller passing through this world, the errant Christian that he was, must have felt sure that, after entering the gates of the Land Below, he would be welcomed into the radiant Mansion of the Supreme Architect. But it is written that "To every thing there is a season, and a time to every purpose under the heaven."

IV

With the arrival of the good weather, Gaudí began to revive and to receive visits from people who showed him solid friendship: among them, Bishop Torras i Bages, who watched over him carefully, and Joaquim Ruyra, the prince of Catalan prose. In Bishop Torras, dignified, severe and short-sighted as he was, Gaudí had a spiritual guide. In the writer Ruyra, prematurely aged, negligently dressed and with dust-covered shoes, he had a fellow pilgrim.

Days, weeks and months passed. The summer began to fade. And with the falling of the leaves and the whistling of the swallows returning to their winter quarters, the architect returned to his house in Barcelona. The learned professor Joan Bassegoda says that it was at this time when, still convalescing, Gaudí drew the western façade of the Temple of the Holy Family.

A gouache drawing which is still conserved reflects, says Bassegoda, "the dramatism of the façade, which commemorates the Death of Christ, drawn by someone who believed he had seen death with his own eyes."

It was plain that the spectre of death had not departed from the Parc Güell. The omens of that Christmas were not good. On 11th January 1912, Rosa Egea i Gaudí died at the age of 36, just one year older than the age at which her mother had passed away.

CHAPTER 19

Cypresses of stone

I

"I understand Gaudí's situation of isolation after the death of his niece, who lived with him. A man who does not seek outward expression nor relations misses those domestic affections, which he now needs to replace with the affection of friendship."

Bishop Torras i Bages wrote these words in a letter to his colleague, the Jesuit priest Ignasi Casanovas. The bishop asked Casanovas to accompany Gaudí to Vic again in attempt to revitalise him a little.

From that moment on, the architect accepted no more new commissions, and on returning to Barcelona he plunged himself fully into the works of the Sagrada Família.

Alone and abandoned, with the sole company of his thoughts, every day the architect walked down to the plain of the Sagrada Família from the hill of the Parc Güell: a good hour downhill and an hour and a half uphill. Sometimes, however, he stayed to sleep on a bed he had improvised in his cabin-like workshop beside the building works of the Temple.

Every week a young woman went to Gaudí's house to do the cleaning. She was a novice who, years later, would enter a religious community, and who observed the details of that nice gentleman who was so neglectful of his clothing. So neglectful and empty of life that he never ate meat and sometimes settled for just a few leaves of lettuce and a glass of milk, following the naturalist recipes of Father Kneipp, as his father had done. So sickly that, to combat his arthritis, his ankles and legs were wrapped in bandages that sometimes hung below his trouser bottoms and made him look like a holy beggar. So lonely and sad, but he never complained, and so good to humble folk, and so devout.

For the novice and future nun, that gentleman was a saint. As much a saint as that St. Anthony of Padua standing in the niche in the entrance hall whom Gaudí saluted every day on leaving and entering the house, taking off his hat, that faded black hat that he always wore.

II

The donations were growing scarce, and there were periods when the works on the Temple were paralysed. At these times Gaudí himself went out in the street to ask for contributions.

Catalonia and Spain had remained neutral during the Great War of 1914-18, but the times were very uncertain. At the end of the War, a German architecture student named Ernst Neufert, anxious to forget the catastrophe and leave behind the northern mists, made a journey to discover the lands south of the Pyrenees. Having decided to stop over in Barcelona, he found a comfortable, sunny guest house away from the centre of the city.

He was a student of the Bauhaus, the school founded by Walter Gropius, the world-famous architect who, at the beginning, had idealised the figure of the old masons, before devoting himself to the mass production of buildings on the basis of the square, the rectangle and the circle.

Neufert's first surprise was when he looked out of his window and saw a row of monumental stone cypress trees rising up towards the clouds. He had expected surprising things of the Latin people, but that construction surpassed all of his expectations.

"It's the Temple of the Holy Family," he was told. "The architect is Mr. Gaudí."

A temple? What kind of architect could be the author of that fantasy? Ernst Neufert was keen to know more. And when he was told that the old architect lived alone, with no family, and that he spent hours shut in his workshop, which looked like a cabin, and that he worked like a traditional craftsman, dedicated totally to planning the future temple, even when the works were stopped due to a lack of funds, Neufert hastened to see for himself.

This is his excited written testimony:

"I saw there the *ideal architect's workshop* that Gropius had spoken of so much in the romantic beginnings of the Bauhaus. There was the authentic *Bauhütte* [the hut of the medieval mason], the cabin built on the firm foundations of faith, which I would not have found in any other place on the planet! It made a profound impression on me, and I felt the desire to talk to Gaudí.

"The architect did not receive visitors, apart from a few church dignitaries. But a Swiss guide gave me to understand that the only way to meet Gaudí was to go to the Cathedral first thing in the morning at the end of the mass. I followed his advice.

"In the first row of pews I saw the architect, kneeling. At the end of the mass, Gaudí left by a side door. I followed him and greeted him, telling him I was an architecture student and an admirer of his work. He smiled and told me to accompany him.

"We walked on side by side, without saying a word. I was nervous, and I couldn't remember a single word of the Spanish I had learned. After a while we began to talk. The buildings we saw along the way had given us a topic of conversation. Gaudí said that *Nature is our great teacher.* I told him of the powerful impression the mountains of Montserrat had made on me when I went there on an outing.

111

"And in that way, walking through the streets of Barcelona, we reached the foot of the Temple of the Holy Family, as the city was waking to a new day. Gaudí looked up at the spires and asked me, "Don't you think that the spires are rather reminiscent of the rocky needles of Montserrat?"

"That meeting with the architect Gaudí was, for my training and for the evolution of my career, one of the most important of my life."

III

With the works on the Sagrada Família stopped, in 1922 a Congress of Architects of the whole Spanish State was held in Barcelona. And it was the Basque architect Teodoro de Anasagasti who said:

"Those of us who have come from far away, admirers of Catalonia, of Barcelona, of the enormous effort of your race ... have seen rising over the city the towering silhouette of those daring spires, the work of Gaudí, that innovative and highly personal artist, that good and honest man. Gaudí labours and creates like an artist of the glorious times. He produces for us and for the triumph of the highest ideals ... If this aspiration which is now rising up towards the sky is to end as tragic ruins, what page of stone will our time have written in the history of Art?"

In those days of decline, Gaudí had been asked when the works of the Temple would be finished. He had replied, "My client is in no hurry."

The novice who did the cleaning in Gaudí's house already knew for what client the architect had been working exclusively in the last few years. Now outsiders were beginning to realise, too. Neufert and Anasagasti were not the only ones.

Sullivan, the designer of revolutionary skyscrapers in Chicago, had been impressed by a series of photographs of Gaudí's Temple in the American magazine *Western Archi-*

tect. He looked at them time and again and concluded, "It is the greatest work of all creative architecture in the last twenty-five years. It is the spiritual representation concealed in the stone itself."

On the other side of the world, in Japan, professor Kenji Imai had decided, while leafing through the British magazine *Builder*, that he would travel to Europe to meet the pioneers of European architecture: Ostberg the Swede, Steiner of Switzerland, and, especially, that enlightened artist in Barcelona who sculpted mysterious forms in stone.

CHAPTER 20

End of the line

I

The rain that had fallen at the end of August had announced the arrival of the bad weather. In the streets leading to the church of Sant Just, close to the Cathedral of Barcelona, there were only long faces to be seen.

It was just after eight o'clock in the morning when Antoni Gaudí, in his eternal black suit and with a scarf round his neck, walked up the four steps of the church. That day, 11th September 1924, a clandestine mass was to be held in memory of the Catalans who had died attempting to defend Barcelona from the attack of the Castilian and French armies on 11th September 1714.

As Gaudí was about to enter the church, an armed policeman stopped him. Although it was only a mass, the atmosphere was unsettled. It was a year since the Andalusian general Miguel Primo de Rivera had staged a *coup d'état*. Catalonia, like the whole Spanish state, was under a military dictatorship.

The conversation between the policeman —who spoke only in Castilian— and the architect —who spoke Catalan throughout— and the events which followed are recorded in a document conserved in the Municipal Historical Archive of Barcelona:

"Where are you going?"
"I'm going to mass."

"You can't go in."

"I'm going in."

"You're not going in!"

And taking Gaudí by the arm, the policeman led him to the police station. The interrogation, in front of four surly officers, was brief.

"What's your name?"

"Antoni Gaudí."

"How old are you?"

"71."

"Profession?"

"Architect."

"Then your profession obliges you to speak in Castilian!"

"My profession obliges me to pay my taxes and I pay them, but not to stop speaking my own language."

"What was your father's name?"

"Francesc Gaudí."

"What do you mean, 'Francesc'?"

One of the other officers growled at Gaudí, "If you weren't an old man I'd smash your face in. Wretch, swine!"

The architect was shut in a dark cell and was told that he would not be released until he paid a fine of 50 pesetas — the equivalent of four days' wages for a skilled worker. Gaudí did not have the money on him, so he sent a message to a priest he knew, the rector of the nearby church of the Mercè.

In fact, Gaudí asked the priest for 75 pesetas. In the cells there was another detained man, a poor Castilian immigrant who sold fruit in the street. The police had confiscated his wares and fined him 25 pesetas, but as he had no way of paying it, he would have to rot in the cells.

When the priest hurried in with the money, Gaudí gave 25 pesetas to the other prisoner, and they both paid their fines and were released. The fruit seller had no idea of the identity of the old, white-bearded man whose first act on entering the cell had been to kneel down on the wet floor and pray. Weeping, the fruit seller asked Gaudí for his name and address, so that he could return the 25 pesetas to him as soon as possible. Gaudí said, "Charity is not to be returned," and took his leave.

II

Early in 1925 Gaudí began to feel that his strength was failing. On 23rd January he made a decision that had been in his mind for some time. He wrote two letters to the Archbishop of Tarragona, expressing his last wishes.

In one document he declared that, "in loving memory of his mother, Antònia Cornet i Bertran", he left established in Reus a pious foundation to finance a practice of devotion to Our Lady of Montserrat. For the maintenance of the foundation he provided 35 bond certificates in the Almansa-Valencia-Tarragona Railway. Gaudí reserved the right, while he lived, to collect the interest on the said capital when the Diocesan Bank paid it. After his death, this interest was to be collected by the rector or priest who was in charge of the foundation.

In the second document, the architect declared that, by inheritance from his father Francesc Gaudí i Serra and his niece Rosa Egea i Gaudí, he owned in Riudoms a house consisting of ground floor, two upper floors and loft, two plots of land with vines and fruit trees, and 6 shares in the Riudecanyes Reservoir Company (created by people from Reus, Riudoms and other towns in order to irrigate their fields), that he transferred these properties and shares to the Archbishop and that the amount deriving from their sale was to be in favour of the Archbishop of Tarragona and the Rector of Riudoms, in order to endow a pious foundation in the parish of Riudoms "in loving memory of and prayer for his Father."

III

Gaudí's circle of good friends included the sculptor Llorenç Matamala, the creator of many of the delicate and harmonious figures of the first façade of the Sagrada Família, that dedicated to the Birth of Christ. And Matamala, seeing Gaudí so drained of life, had often accompanied him in the evening to his remote and lonely house in the Parc Güell, and had even occasionally spent the night there in order not to leave him alone. But the situation could not last much longer.

Matamala had a wife and children, and although he was four years younger than Gaudí, he too was getting old and was not in the best of health. At the beginning of the winter of 1925, Matamala fell seriously ill. Gaudí decided to stop walking between the Parc Güell and the Sagrada Família each day. From then on he spent every night in the iron bed he had had placed in a corner of his workshop next to the Temple.

Matamala died at Christmas. Gaudí was more alone than ever.

IV

In the evenings, in the dim light of the oil lamps, the shadows of the strange objects hanging from the ceiling crept up and down the walls of the workshop.

Meanwhile, outside, the trunks of the old trees in the Gardens of Seven Secrets grew slowly and became the columns of the Temple, "with the creative slowness of the beginnings of the world."

Gaudí was walking uncertainly and distractedly in the street that afternoon of 7th June 1926, and he neither saw nor heard the tram bearing down on him.

He died in the hospital for the poor two days later. All they found were, in one pocket, a handful of currants and peanuts, and in the other, a crumpled book: the Gospels.

EPILOGUE

Antoni Gaudí was buried in the crypt of the Temple of the Holy Family of Barcelona.

His tomb was profaned during the Spanish Civil War of 1936-39.

After his death, his childhood friend Eduard Toda promoted the restoration of the Monastery of Poblet, as they had dreamed as boys.

In the 1960's, Professor George R. Collins of Columbia University wrote, "For Gaudí, the theory of architecture was inseparable from the analysis of the laws of nature and of religious symbolism. What Gaudí did was to render homage to the One, the Supreme Being."

The architect Jordi Bonet i Armengol said, in 1993, "Starting with George R. Collins, the interest in Catalan architecture in the U.S.A. has increased, and Gaudí has come to be considered as one of the great creators of world architecture."

During Gaudí's life, his work had many detractors and was considered outdated. In the present day, the Swiss-based Spanish engineer and architect Santiago Calatrava, whose designs are in great demand with the aesthetic avant-garde, confesses to the influence of Gaudinian conceptions.

On 7th November 1982, Pope John Paul II visited Barcelona and declared, during a mass held before the Sagrada Família, "The Church is the universal home of the family of God, your home. To be the visible expression of this mysterious reality is the vocation of this magnificent Temple of the Holy Family of Barcelona, which we owe to the inspiration of Father Josep Manyanet and the artistic genius of Antoni Gaudí."

In the summer of 1998, the Archbishop of Barcelona, Ricard Maria Carles, with the support of all of the bishops of Catalonia, announced the decision to initiate the process of beatification of Gaudí.

The 150th anniversary of the birth of Antoni Gaudí i Cornet falls on 25th June 2002.

NOTES ON CHAPTERS

Chapter 1

Various contemporaries of Gaudí coincided in recording that, in the last years of his life, the architect dressed like a poor man. The cartoonist Feliu Elias Bracons, who signed as 'Apa', satirised Gaudí as a stooped old man dressed in a threadbare jacket, crumpled trousers and worn-out shoes. This caricature appeared in the Barcelona newspaper *La Publicitat* on 11th June 1926, the day before the architect's burial.

The reference to the Japanese professor Kenji Imai appears in the article '*The visit of Professor Kenji Imai to Barcelona in the year 1926 to meet Gaudí*', by Masayuki Irie (Biblioteca de la Càtedra Gaudí, Av. de Pedralbes, Barcelona).

Chapter 2

The etymology of the German *Gaud* or *God* was defended by Francesc de B. Moll in *Els llinatges catalans* (Mallorca, 1987).

On German etymologies and their diffusion in Catalonia between the 9th and 11th centuries, there is a clarifying study by Enric Moreu-Rey, who was a professor of the University of Barcelona, in *Antroponímia. Història dels nostres prenoms, cognoms i renoms* (Publicacions de la Universitat de Barcelona, 1991).

However, attention must be drawn here to the erroneous etymology of the surname Gaudí given by the eminent Catalan linguist Joan Coromines, ex-professor of the University of Chicago. In his *Diccionari Etimològic i Complementari de la Llengua Catalana*, Coromines said that the surname Gaudí comes from "*Gaudints*, a name traditionally given in Lleida to men of studies" and/or from "*gaudins*, the principal fellowship of the Cathedral of Solsona". Coromines was apparently unaware of the Occitan origin of Gaudí's ancestors, which is explained in Chapter 3 of this book, otherwise he would have made a different analysis of the question.

The Gaudís, Gaudys or Gaudins of Europe (obvious variants of the same surname) are glossed in the majority of great European encyclopaedias: *Encyclopédie Française*, *Enciclopedia Espasa*, etc.

The etymology of the toponym Cornet which I give here is taken from the *Onomasticon Cataloniae* by Prof. Joan Coromines.

The Cornet lineage was studied by my great-uncle Gabriel Castellà i Raich (1876-1959), historian and archivist of the town of Igualada and correspondent member of the Academy of Letters of Barcelona. In 1929 he published, in nº 1 of the *Revista d'Igualada*, a research article entitled '*Nissagues il.lustres d'Igualada: Cornet*' ('*Illustrious Families of Igualada: Cornet*'). In February 1948 he published an article on the coat of arms of the Cornet family in the Bulletin of the Igualada Photography Society.

Chapter 3

Gaudí's Occitan origin was discovered in the 1930's, after his death, by a private genealogical researcher, Josep Maria Armengol i Viver. By investigating the parish archives, Mr. Armengol was able to establish the family tree of the ancestors of the future architect, on both the paternal and maternal sides. He published the findings of his investigations in an article entitled *La gènesi de Gaudí* which, accompanied by the family tree, was published in the Barcelona newspaper *El Matí* on 21st June 1936.

Other people interested in the topic have subsequently added collateral branches and other elements to the tree established by Mr. Armengol. The Associació d'Amics de Gaudí of Reus offers to send a copy to anyone requesting it.

Chapter 4

The cottage on the Mas de la Calderera farm was reformed and enlarged after Gaudí's death. The description of the cottage as it was during the architect's life is taken from the declarations made before a notary by Rosa Domingo i Giol, a resident of Riudoms who had been the tenant of the farm from 1921 to 1926. Her description was published in the book *Defensa de Gaudí* by J.M. Guix Sugranyes (1st edition Reus, 1960; 2nd edition Reus, 1978).

On Gaudí's arthritic illness, his stays at the Mas de la Calderera farm and the influence of nature on his childhood spirit, there is the testimony of the architect Joan Bergós i Massó (1894-1974), who was 32 years old and one of Gaudí's assistants when the latter died. Mr. Bergós published his memories of his friend and teacher in the book *Antoni Gaudí, l'home i l'obra* (Catalan edition by Ariel, Barcelona, 1954; Castilian edition by Universitat Politècnica de Barcelona, Barcelona, 1974).

Chapter 5

The influence of his father's trade of coppersmith on Gaudí's work was pointed out by the first students of his work, whether contemporaries of his or of a later generation.

123

The late Professor George R. Collins of Columbia University, the author of various works on Gaudí, specified: "The speciality of the house (the father's workshop) were tubes for liquor distilleries. In his old age Gaudí said that his sense of space began to evolve in his father's workshop, among the winding copper tubes, which bear a certain resemblance to the complicated geometries and spirals of Gaudí's art." See G.R. Collins, *Gaudí*, Braziller (New York, 1960).

In Catalan there is a text signed by George R. Collins and Josep M. Ballarín, published in Volume 3 of *La nostra gent; Història de Catalunya* (Plaza & Janés, Barcelona)

Professor G.R. Collins died at the age of 75 in Falmouth, Massachusetts, in January 1993.

Gaudí's childhood period as an apprentice in the factory of the Vapor Nou in Reus is related by Jordi Elias in his work *Gaudí. Assaig biogràfic*, Ediciones Circo (Barcelona, 1961).

From the same book is the anecdote that a woman from the Gaudí-Cornet family sometimes went to collect leftover food from neighbours. This anecdote was related to Jordi Elias in around 1960 by Roser Segimon of Reus, the widow of Pere Milà i Camps.

The project of reconstructing the Monastery of Poblet is related in detail in the book by Joan Bergós i Massó.

The quotations from Eduard Toda, one of Gaudí's partners in the Poblet project, are reproduced in the book by J. Elias.

Chapter 6

I have based my account of the crisis of the Papal States on the work by Charles Petrie, *Diplomatic History* (London, 1944).

The quotation from Oswald Spengler is from the final chapter of *Der Untergang des Abendlandes (The Decline of the West)*.

The evolution of the name Josep in Catalonia is analysed by E. Moreu-Rey in *Antroponímia, op. cit.*

Marie-Paule Demarré is the author of the paper *Le capitaine Henri-Hubert Belletable (1813-1855), fondateur de l'Association de la Sainte Famille a Lièges (Belgique)*, which is to be published in the minutes of the 4TH INTERNATIONAL CONGRESS ON THE HOLY FAMILY, organised in Begues (Barcelona) by the congregation Fills de la Sagrada Família, Jesús, Maria i Josep, founded by Father Josep Manyanet. The address of the congregation is: Carrer Entença 301, 08029 Barcelona, Catalonia, Spain. Tel.: 93 439 4305, fax: 93 430 4303.

The biographical data on Father Manyanet are taken from the book by J.M. Blanquet and J. Piquer *José Manyanet. Profeta de la familia*, Biblioteca de Autores Cristianos (Madrid, 1974).

The quotations from Josep Pla are from his book *Homenots, Primera sèrie*, Editorial Selecta (Barcelona, 1958-1962).

The quotations from Graham Greene are to be found in his *Catholic Essays*.

The references to Alexis Carrel proceed basically from the article by Alain Ledoux *Alexis Carrel*, published in *Science et Vie* (Paris, September 1973).

The apparition of the Virgin in Knock, Ireland, in 1879 is described in the article by Kenneth L. Woodward *Hail Mary*, published in *Newsweek* magazine, August 25, 1997.

The prediction that the architect of the Sagrada Família would have blue eyes was related by Josep Pijoan to Josep Pla, who recorded it in his work *Homenots*, op. cit.

Chapter 7

Joan Bassegoda i Nonell is the contemporary Catalan architect who has accumulated the most documentation and published the most writings about the work of Gaudí, also referring to documented aspects of his life. Professor Bassegoda's most voluminous book on these matters is *El*

Gran Gaudí, Editorial Ausa (Sabadell, 1989), which has been used as a general reference for this chapter.

The leaflet circulating in Barcelona in 1871 is mentioned by the historians J. Termes and A. Colomines in *Les Bases de Manresa de 1892 i els origens del catalanisme,* Generalitat de Catalunya (Barcelona, 1992).

The quotation from Hans Christian Andersen is translated from *Viaje por España,* Alianza Editorial (Madrid, 1988) in the Catalan version given by Pere Balañà in *Visió cosmopolita de Catalunya,* Generalitat de Catalunya (Barcelona, 1991).

References to Gaudí's military service are conserved in the District Historical Archive of Reus. An annotation from the year 1874 in the book of records of call-ups to the Municipal Council of Reus reads: "Antonio Gaudí y Cornet has not reported, and no-one has claimed any exemption for him. In view of which the Illustrious Municipal Council ... has declared him a soldier."

The facial characteristics of Francesc Gaudí i Cornet, the architect's elder brother, can be observed in the portrait which appears in the sheet of photographs of the students of the Faculty of Medicine of Barcelona of the year 1872, reproduced by J.M. Guix Sugranyes in *Defensa de Gaudí* (Reus, 1960).

As for the date when Francesc Gaudí finished his medical studies, I have been guided by the letter signed on 6th September 1954 by the then Dean of the Faculty of Medicine of Barcelona, Dr. A. Pedro i Pons, also reproduced by Guix Sugranyes in the above work.

The reference to the marriage of Rosa, the elder daughter of the Gaudí family, is from Bergós.

Chapter 8

Gaudí's diaries were published by Enric Casanelles: *Nueva visión de Gaudí,* (Barcelona, 1965).

The information on Salvador Pagés' supposed stay in the U.S.A. was published in 1961 by J. Elias in *Gaudí, Assaig biogràfic*, and in 1975 by Josep M. Moreu and his son Enric Moreu-Rey in the magazine *Serra d'Or* (Barcelona, 15 May 1975).

The data referring to the cooperative La Obrera Mataronesa are from the book by J. Pomés and Maria Rodríguez *L'Obrera Mataronesa*, Caixa d'Estalvis Laietana (Mataró, 1997).

On the illness and the readings of the Reus writer Joaquim Maria Bartrina, I have been guided by the information given by Ramon Sumoy in the corresponding entry in the *Gran Enciclopèdia Catalana* (Barcelona, 1971). As for Bartrina's activities in Mataró, these are referred to in *L'Obrera Mataronesa, op. cit.*

Chapter 9

The quotations from the American professor Lewis Mumford are from his book *The Culture of the Cities*, first published in the U.S.A. in 1928.

Concerning Gaudí's urban plan for the cooperative La Obrera Mataronesa, a copy of the plans is conserved in the Historical Archive of Mataró, in the box classified AH-0233 (pp. 15 and 16).

A dossier in the same Archive conserves some original documents, such as applications to the Mayor signed by Salvador Pagés, and the replies and the planning permits issued by the Municipal Council.

A description of the standard which Gaudí designed for the cooperative can be found in Elias, *op. cit.*

Chapter 10

Bergós and other authors testify to the excellent physical health of Gaudí's father.

The speculations of the writer Carles Soldevila on Gaudí's youthful romances are found in the book *Figures de Catalunya*, Aedos, (1st edition Barcelona, 1955, 2nd edition Barcelona, 1962).

Elias, *op. cit.*, refers to the memories, more or less distorted, of these matters still conserved by some collateral relatives in the mid-20th century.

Josep M. Moreu i Fornells (1873-1961) left part of his memoirs in writing. Another part was tape-recorded by his son Enric Moreu-Rey (1917-1992), a Doctor of Letters of the University of Barcelona. Dr. Moreu-Rey published a résumé of this material under the title *Gaudí a Mataró* in the magazine *Serra d'Or* (Barcelona, 15 May 1975).

Chapter 11

The sources of this chapter are basically from the previously-mentioned memoirs of Josep M. Moreu i Fornells, augmented with some details or clarifications by his son Enric Moreu-Rey.

'Allen Kardec' was the pseudonym of the Frenchman Léon Rivail, who in 1857, at the age of 54, wrote —in 'automatic writing' as the spiritualists say— *Le livre des esprits*, which was translated into many languages and had an extraordinary resonance.

The failure of the cooperative La Obrera Mataronesa is related in detail in *L'Obrera Mataronesa, op. cit.*

Chapter 12

Eduard Fontseré i Mestre's membership of the Masons is documented in the book by Pere Sánchez *La maçoneria a Catalunya, 1868-1936*, published by the Barcelona City Council and Edicions 62 (Barcelona, 1990), and, by the same author, *La lògia Lealtad: un exemple de maçoneria catalana (1869-1939)*, Ed. Altafulla (Barcelona, 1985).

Eudald Canibell's membership of the Masons is also documented in the first of the above books.

A complete list of the many books published by Eudald Canibell appears in the corresponding entry in the *Enciclopedia Espasa*.

Certain unpublished memoirs of Canibell, in which he refers to the threats of La Mano Negra, are mentioned by the Austrian anarchist Max Nettlau (1865-1944) in his posthumously-published work *La Première Internationale en Espagne* (Dordrecht, Netherlands, 1969).

The incident with La Mano Negra is quoted by the Argentinian Hispanicist Clara E. Lida in her book *Anarquismo y revolución en la España del XIX*, Siglo XXI de España Editores (Madrid, 1971).

Gaudí's attendance at a discussion group of anticlerical intellectuals was reported by Josep Pla in his book *Homenots*, op. cit.

The quotations from the Russian writer Pavlovski appear in *Visió cosmopolita de Catalunya* by Pere Balañà, *op. cit.*

Chapter 13

The most recent and complete work on the architect Joan Martorell i Montells is the doctoral thesis by Jaume Aymar, Doctor in History of Art and Dean of the Ecclesiastical Faculty of Philosophy of Catalonia (c. Diputació 231, 08007 Barcelona).

The information on the Güell Estate is taken from *El Gran Gaudí* by J. Bassegoda, *op. cit.* On the family ties of the Güell family, there is good documentation in the National Archive of Catalonia in Sant Cugat del Vallès.

On the activity of the slaver Antonio López López, the book *Catalunya a Cuba*, Barcino (Barcelona, 1988) by Joaquim Roy, professor of the University of Miami, gives a neutral vision. For a defamatory view, it is very interesting to read the booklet *La verdadera vida de Antonio López y López* (Barcelona, 1855) by F. Bru, who was his brother-in-law.

The comments by George R. Collins on Gaudí's different artistic periods are taken from his article on Gaudí in *The New Encyclopaedia Britannica*, 15th Edition (Chicago, 1992).

Chapter 14

For the source of the prediction concerning blue eyes, see the note corresponding to Chapter 6.

Father Llorenç Riber i Campins was born in 1881 in Mallorca, where he entered, as a page, the service of the Bishop, also named Campins. Riber stood out as a Baroque writer in Catalan. The sentence of his that I mention comes from *Antoni Gaudí, la seva vida, les seves obres, la seva mort*, Ed. Poliglota (Barcelona, 1926), quoted by Jordi Castellanos in *Intel.lectuals, cultura i poder*, Edicions de la Magrana (Barcelona, 1998).

Miquel Ramon Ferrà i Juan was born in Mallorca in 1885, the son of a mason and archaeologist. He studied Philosophy and Letters at the University of Barcelona. He excelled in art theory and in the translation into Catalan of French and Italian poets.

The quotation from Ferrà on Gaudí is taken from *La cultura contemporània a Catalunya (1888-1931)* by Edmon Vallès, published by La Caixa de Catalunya i Balears (Barcelona, 1997).

Chapter 15

The stories about Gaudí's discrepancies with his clients have been related by numerous authors. The most explicit is J. Elias, *op. cit.*

As for Gaudí's discrepancies with the Castilian clergy of Astorga, some authors have preferred to see only the architect's difficult personality. In contrast, Rafael Álvarez Izquierdo, in his book *Gaudí*, underlines the hostility existing in Astorga towards the Catalans.

The references to the Godó family from Igualada are taken from the *Diccionari Biogràfic d'Igualadins* by M.A. Bisbal and M.T. Miret. The marriage of Josep Batlló to a woman of the Godó family is deduced from their family tree, established by Armand de Fluvià.

On Josep Guardiola, there is a biographical reference in the *Diccionari dels Catalans d'Amèrica.*

The quotation from the journalist Jaume Bofill i Mates appeared in the newspaper *La Publicitat* in 1930, and is cited by Jordi Castellanos in *Intel.lectuals, cultura i poder, op. cit.*

The quotation from the art historian and ecclesiastic Manuel Trens also appeared in the newspaper *La Publicitat*, in a 1926 article written after Gaudí's death, and it is also cited by Castellanos.

Chapter 16

The declaration by Roberto Pane is mentioned by J. Bassegoda in an article on the Parc Güell published in the Bulletin of the Reial Acadèmia de Belles Arts de Sant Jordi.

Numerous authors have related the comments made about Gaudí's work in the Chicago office of Louis Henry Sullivan.

Gaudí's fast during the Lent of 1894 was related by the artist Ricard Opisso, a contemporary of the architect, in the *Diari de Barcelona* of 24th March 1951.

The physical characteristics of the clergyman Torras i Bages are taken textually from a description of him by the journalist Carles Soldevila in his book *Figures de Catalunya, op. cit.*

On Gaudí's father's enjoyment of life there is a reference by Prof. Pijoan, reported by Josep Pla, and others by J. Elias.

Details of the Gaudí family's move from Carrer Diputació to the Parc Güell can be found in the book *Gaudí* by Josep F. Ràfols, Ed. Canosa (Barcelona, 1928).

There was nothing esoteric about Sebastian Kneipp's naturalistic practices, as they were based on popular medicine. Born in 1821 in Stephansried, Germany, and very delicate in health, he trained as a priest. It was in the parish of Wörishofen where he publicised his therapeutic system, based on water baths associated with medicinal plants. Kneipp died in 1897.

At present, Laboratoris Fher, S.A., of Barcelona commercialises, under the name of Kneipp, sweets containing *Valeriana officialis*, a medicinal herb very well known in Catalan popular medicine, and indicated for nerves, anxiety, insomnia, etc.

Chapter 17

The reference to the 'Day of the Beast' is from the Book of Revelation, chapters IX and XI.

The saying "bread and onion is enough for the workers" ("Els obrers, amb *pa i ceba* en tenen prou") is attributed to an Igualada businessman of the late 19th and early 20th centuries, whose house has been known ever since as 'Cal Pa i Ceba'. The anecdote which gave rise to the nickname is documented in the book *Renoms igualadins* (Igualada, 1984).

The reference to Leo XIII's 'holy rage' is from Graham Greene, as is the story about the Bishop of San Luís de Potosí.

The description of the Catalans by Henry Havelock Ellis is from his book *The Soul of Spain* (London, 1908).

The information about Lerroux is included in the doctoral thesis of Prof. J.B. Culla, *El lerrouxisme a Catalunya.*

The details about Gaudí's stay at Can Rocafiguera in Vic are reported by Josep Pla, *op. cit.*

Chapter 18

The characteristics of the illness of Gaudí's niece are mentioned in *Gaudí, l'home i l'obra* by J. Bergós, *op. cit.* As for her date of death, I have taken that given by Joan Bassegoda.

Gaudí's house in the Parc Güell was converted into the Gaudí House-Museum in 1963. Mr. Josep M. Garrut was its director for some time, and some of the stories about the architect's life there are owed to him.

Gaudí made his will before the notary public of Puigcerdà, Ramon Cantó, according to a certificate of the General Registry of Deeds of Last Will and Testament, depending on the Ministry of Justice, in Madrid. The Notarial Archive of Puigcerdà was destroyed during the Spanish Civil War.

The quotation "To every thing there is a season..." is from Ecclesiastes, III, 1.

Chapter 19

The fragment of the letter written by Bishop Torras i Bages is taken from *Relíquies literàries* by Ignasi Casanovas, quoted by J. Castellanos, *op. cit.*

The mentions of the novice are taken from declarations by Mr. J.M. Garrut (see notes to Chapter 18).

Ernst Neufert was, in the 1960's, a professor of the Technische Hochschule in Darmstadt, Germany, where he often spoke to his students about 'good old' Gaudí. A Catalan student of his, Joaquim de Vilar-Vergés, asked him for a written testimony of his memories of Gaudí, which he sent to Enric Casanelles, who published some fragments of them in *Nueva visión de Gaudí* (Barcelona, 1965).

The quotation of Teodoro de Anasagasti is taken from J. Bassegoda.

The comments by L.H. Sullivan and Kenji Imai are taken from the article by Masayuki Irie, *op. cit.*

Chapter 20

On Gaudí's detention, the section 'Miscellaneous Documents' of the Municipal Historical Archive of Barcelona contains a number of unsigned typewritten sheets with this sentence at the end: "This, almost textually, is what was told to me by Mr. Valls." The document was reproduced *in extenso* by Joan Crexell in the magazine *Serra d'Or* in September 1987.

Gaudí's donations to the Archbishop of Tarragona are reproduced from *Defensa de Gaudí* by J.M. Guix Sugranyes, *op. cit.*

The phrase "with the creative slowness of the beginnings of the world" is from Manuel Trens.

BIBLIOGRAPHY

ÁLVAREZ IZQUIERDO, Rafael: *Gaudí*. Ed. Palabra (Madrid 1992).

AYMAR, Jaume: *L'arquitecte Jaume Martorell i Montells* (unpublished doctoral thesis). Copy existing in Biblioteca de la Càtedra Gaudí (Barcelona 1998).

BALAÑA, Pere: *Visió cosmopolita de Catalunya*. Generalitat de Catalunya (Barcelona 1991).

BARAUT, Cebrià; BLANQUET, J. M. i SÁNCHEZ, A.: *José Mañanet, apóstol de la família y de la juventud*. Hijos de la Sagrada Família (Barcelona 1969).

BASSEGODA I NONELL, Joan: *El gran Gaudí*. Ed. Ausa (Sabadell 1989).

— *Gaudí, arquitectura del futur*. La Caixa/Salvat (Barcelona 1984).

BERGOS, Joan: *Gaudí. L'home i l'obra*. Ed. Ariel (Barcelona 1954). There is a Spanish-language edition published by the Universitat Politècnica de Barcelona (Barcelona 1974).

BLANQUET, J. M. I PIQUER, J.: *José Manyanet, profeta de la família*. BAC popular (Madrid 1984).

BOFILL, Rafael M.: *L'arquitectura nacional de Catalunya*. Ed. La Magrana (Barcelona, 1998).

CARR, Raymond: *Spain 1808-1939*. Oxford University Press (1966).

CASANELLES, Enric: *Nueva visión de Gaudí* (Barcelona 1965).

CASTELLANOS, Jordi: *Gaudí, arquitecte de Déu*, in "Intel·lectuals, cultura i poder". Ed. La Magrana (Barcelona 1998).

COLLINS, George R.: *Gaudí*. Braziller (Nova York 1960).

CULLA. Joan B.: *El lerrouxisme a Catalunya* (Barcelona 1986).

ELIAS, Jordi: *Gaudí. Assaig biogràfic*. Ed.Circo (Barcelona 1961).

ELLIS, Havelock: *The Soul of Spain* (London 1908).

FEBRES-VALLFOGONA-MARINGALLO: *Renoms igualadins*. Omnium Cultural (Igualada 1984).

GREENE, Graham: *Ensayos católicos.* Emecé (Buenos Aires, Argentina, 1955).

GUIX SUGRANYES, J. M.: *Defensa de Gaudí.* 2nd. edition. Ed. Monterols (Reus 1978).

HALÉVY, Élie: *Histoire du socialisme européen.* Librairie Gallimard (Paris 1948).

KOESTLER, Arthur: *The Act of Creation. Penguin Books/Arkana* (London 1989).

— *The Roots of Coincidence.* Hutchinson of London (London 1972).

LIDA, Clara E.: *Anarquismo y revolución en la España del siglo XIX* . Siglo XXI de España Editores (Madrid 1972).

LLARCH, Joan: *Gaudí, biografía mágica.* Plaza & Janés (Barcelona 1982).

MARTINELL I BRUNET, Cèsar: *L'arquitecte Gaudí.* Ajuntament de Barcelona (Barcelona 1976).

MARTINELL, Cèsar: *Gaudí. His life.* Edited by G. Collins (Cambridge, Mass.USA,1975).

— *Gaudí i la Sagrada Família* (Barcelona 1951).

MOREU-REY, Enric: *Antroponímia.* Publicacions Universitat de Barcelona (Barcelona 1991).

MUMFORD, Lewis: *The Culture of the Cities* (1928). There is an edition in Argentinian Spanish, by C.M.Reyles: "La cultura de las ciudades". Emecé Ed. (Buenos Aires, s.d.)

PANE, Roberto: *Gaudí.* Ed. di Communità (Milano, 1962/1964).

PETRIE, Sir Charles: *Diplomatic History.* There is a Spanish-language edition by L. de Giralt (Barcelona 1947).

PLA, Josep: *Homenots 2.* Ed.62 (Barcelona 1987).

POMÉS, Salvador i RODRIGUEZ, Maria: *La Obrera Mataronesa.* Caixa d'Estalvis Laietana (Mataró 1997).

RAFOLS, Josep F.: *Gaudí.* Ed.Canosa (Barcelona 1928).

ROJO, Eduardo: *Antoni Gaudí, aquest desconegut:el Parc Güell.* A. Romero, Editora (St Cugat del Vallès 1986).

ROY, Joaquim: *Catalunya a Cuba.* Ed.Barcino (Barcelona 1988).

RUSKIN, John: *The Lamp of Beauty: writings on art.* Selected and edited by Joan Evans. Phaidon Press (London 1995).

— *Ética del barro.* Translated from the English by Elisa Morales de Giner. Ed.Renacimiento (Madrid 1917).

SÁNCHEZ, Pere: *La maçoneria a Catalunya.1868-1936.* Ajuntament de Barcelona/Ed.62 (Barcelona 1990).

SOLDEVILA, Carles: *Figures de Catalunya.* Ed.Aedos (Barcelona 1962).

136

TERMES, J. I COLOMINES, A.: *Les Bases de Manresa de 1892 i els orígens del catalanisme.* Generalitat de Catalunya (Barcelona 1992).

TRUETA, Josep: *L'esperit de Catalunya.* Ed. Selecta (Barcelona 1985).

VALLÉS, Edmon: *La cultura contemporània a Catalunya.* La Caixa (Barcelona 1977).

La Verdad sobre Gaudí: conjunto de pruebas que revalidan el hecho histórico del nacimiento de Gaudí en el "Mas de la Calderera" de Riudoms. Agrupación Cultural de Amigos de Gaudí (s.n.) (Barcelona 1960).

* * *

Diccionari dels catalans d'Amèrica. Generalitat de Catalunya (Barcelona 1992).

Diccionari biogràfic d'Igualadins de Maria Antònia BISBAL i Ma Teresa MIRET. Fundació S. Vives i Casajuana (Barcelona 1986).

Diccionari etimològic i complementari de la llengua catalana, de Joan COROMINES.Curial/La Caixa (Barcelona 1980).

Diccionari català-valencià-balear. D'A. M. ALCOVER-F de B. MOLL. Ed. MOLL (Palma de Mallorca 1978).

Enciclopedia Espasa.

Gran Enciclopèdia Catalana.

The New Encyclopaedia Britannica. Micropaedia (Chicago, USA, 1992).

La Bíblia, interdenominational translation. Associació Bíblica de Catalunya. Ed. Claret. Societats Bíbliques Unides (Barcelona 1994).

* * *

ARTICLES AND TREATISES

ALMUZARA PÉREZ, José Manuel: *Pequeño-gran hombre.* "Diari de Tarragona" (3-XI-1998).

ALOS, Ernest: *Gaudí fa un altre pas cap als altars.* Newspaper "El Periódico" (Barcelona, 2-X-1998).

ARAGAY, Ignasi: *Gaudí per partida doble.* Newspaper "Avui" (Barcelona, 7-XI-1996).

Architecture in accord with Natural Law. Maharishi Global Construction, L·L.C. (Fairfield, Iowa, USA).

BASSEGODA I NONELL, Joan: *Gaudinisme als Estats Units*, in "Jornades d'Estudis Catalano-Americans", Vol. IV. Generalitat de Catalunya (Barcelona 1992).

— *El Park Güell, mitologia i nacionalisme* in the Newsletter of the Reial Acadèmia Catalana de Belles Arts de St Jordi, n°. XI (Barcelona 1997).

BERGOS, Joan; TODA Eduard; SERRAHIMA, Lluís; TRENS, Manuel; ROIG I RAVENTOS, J.; SUGRANYES, D.; LLONGUERES, Joan; NAVARRO, Antoni; articles in *Suplement Gaudí*. Newspaper "El Matí" (Barcelona, 21 -VI- 1936).

Centenari Joan Bergós. Departament de Cultura. Generalitat de Catalunya (Barcelona 1994).

BONET I ARMENGOL, Jordi: *George R. Collins*, in "Jornades d'Estudis Catalano-Americans", Vol. V. Generalitat de Catalunya (Barcelona 1997).

— *Experimentació tecnològica sobre l'arquitectura de Gaudí a la Sagrada Família* in the Newsletter of the Reial Acadèmia Catalana de Belles Arts de Sant Jordi, n°. XI (Barcelona 1997).

BONET I ARMENGOL, mossèn Lluís: *Creo que será fácil demostrar la santidad del arquitecto de la Sagrada Família*. Newspaper "La Vanguardia" (Barcelona, 13-IX-1998).

BONET I GARI, Lluís: *Les quatre conferències sobre En Gaudí i la seva obra al Círcol Artístic de Sant Lluc* (Barcelona).

CABRÉ, Jordi: *La Iglesia catalana se muestra a favor de la beatificación de Gaudí*. "Diari de Tarragona" (Tarragona, 8 -V-1998).

CARANDELL, Josep Maria: *El enigma Gaudí*. Newspaper "La Vanguardia" (Barcelona, 4-X-1998).

CARLES, Cardinal Ricard M.: *Hacia la beatificación de Gaudí*. Newspaper "La Vanguardia" (Barcelona, 23-VIII-1998).

CASTELLAR-GASSOL, J.: *Gaudí, el visionari del Temple*. "Sagrada Família Informació" (Barcelona, May 1995).

CASTELLA I RAICH, Gabriel: *Nissagues il·lustres d'Igualada: Cornet*. Dins "Revista d'Igualada". N.° 1 (Igualada, June 1929).

— *Blasón de la família Cornet*. Newsletter of the Agrupación Fotográfica de Igualada (Igualada, February 1948).

CREXELL, Joan: *Detenció de Gaudí l'11 de setembre de 1924*. Serra d'Or. N.° 335 (Barcelona, September 1987).

COLLINS, George Roseborough: *The Archive of Catalan Art and Architecture. Friends of Gaudí, USA*. Columbia University (New York City, December 1983).

138

COLLINS, George R. i BALLARIN, Josep M.: *Antoni Gaudí i Cornet*, in "La nostra gent". Plaza & Janés, editors (Esplugues de Llobregat 1988).

Engineering: in need of heroes / Why are architects glamorous and engineers anonymous?. "The Economist" (London, May 16th 1998).

FAULI, Josep: *La silueta de Barcelona*. Newspaper "Avui" (Barcelona, 31-V-1998).

FORTUNY TORRES, Xavier: *Manca de veritat històrica sobre Gaudí*. "Diari de Tarragona" (13-XII-1998).

GALOBART SOLER, Josep, monjo de Montserrat: *La Lliga y Gaudí en Montserrat*. "La Vanguardia" (28-VI-1998).

FONTOVA, Rosario: *La Sagrada Família tindrà la torre més alta de Barcelona*. "El Periódico" (Barcelona 11-XI-1997).

Gaudí, arquitecte de Déu. Newsletter. Associació pro beatificació d'Antoni Gaudí/Fundació Catalunya Cristiana (Barcelona 1996).

GIRALT-MIRACLE, Daniel: *La Pedrera. Form and Contents of a Building*. In "La Pedrera". Fundació Caixa Catalunya (Barcelona 1998).

IRIE, Masayuki: *La visita del profesor Kenji Imai a Barcelona, el año 1926, para conocer a Gaudí* (Biblioteca de la Càtedra Gaudí, Barcelona).

LEDOUX, Alain: *Alexis Carrel*. "Science et Vie" (Paris, September 1973).

LLORENS I GRAU, Josep: *L'àvia materna de l'arquitecte Antoni Gaudí era filla de Tarragona*. Diari de Tarragona (13-VII-1998).

MOREU I FORNELLS, Josep M. i MOREU-REY, Enric: *Gaudí a Mataró*. "Serra d'Or".Núm.188 (Barcelona, 15-V-1975).

Orientación adecuada de los edificios. "Notícias MT". Fundación MT (Madrid, September 1997).

PALAU RAFECAS Salvador" *Els molins fariners i les masies del municipi de Les Piles*. In "Recull". n°. 4. Associació Cultural Baixa Segarra-Santa Coloma de Queralt (Santa Coloma de Queralt 1993).

PERMANYER, Lluís: *Antoni Gaudí, the Man*. In "La Pedrera".Fundació Caixa Catalunya (Barcelona 1998).

PITARCH, M.Teresa: *Antoni Gaudí i Cornet és natural de Reus*. "Diari de Tarragona" (19-XI-1998). "La Publicitat". Newspaper (Barcelona, 11-VI-1926).

REQUENA, David: *El Modernismo catalán es anterior al Art Nouveau francés /Expertos en la obra de Antoni Gaudí celebran las V Jornadas en el Palau Bofarull/*. "Diari de Tarragona" (13-XI-1998).

ROHRER, Judith C.:*Una visió apropiada: el Temple de la Sagrada Família de Gaudí i la política arquitectònica de la Lliga Regionalista*, in "Gaudí i el seu temps", edited by J. J.Lahuerta. Ed.Barcanova (Barcelona 1990).

VILLALOBOS, Andrea: *Una obra de Gaudí en Chile*. Diari "El Mercurio" (Santiago de Chile, 2-XI-1997).

VILLAVERDE, Ana: *Comencen el polèmic enderroc de l'antiga seu de la Cooperativa Obrera Mataronense*. Newspaper "El Punt". Edició del Maresme (Mataró 3-X-1998).

WINTERHALDER, Albert: *La casa-museu de Gaudí, oblidada de la mà de Déu*. "Xarxa" (Barcelona, January 1988).

WOODEARD, Kenneth L.: *Hail, Mary*. "Newsweek" (New York, August 25, 1997).

ACKNOWLEDGEMENTS

It would not have been possible to write a book of this nature without consulting a great variety of documentation contained in archives, centres and libraries. I am pleased to make note here of the assistance which I have received in this task from the directors of the following centres:

Study Centre, Riudoms.
Historical Archive of Riudoms.
Historical Archive of Reus.
Friends of Gaudí, Reus.
Library of the Roca i Galés Foundation, Barcelona.
Library of the Association of Architects of Catalonia, Barcelona.
Department of Culture, Reus City Council.
Caixa de Catalunya Foundation, La Pedrera, Barcelona.
Historical Archive of Mataró.
Robafaves Bookshop, Mataró.
La Formiga d'Or Bookshop, Barcelona.
Library of Catalonia, Barcelona.
Fornas Collection, Library of the Parliament of Catalonia, Barcelona.
Centre of Gaudí Studies, Barcelona.
Municipal Historical Archive of Barcelona.
Polytechnic University of Catalonia, Barcelona.
Salvador Vilaseca District Museum, Reus.
Parish of the Sagrada Família, Barcelona.
Gaudí Professorship, Barcelona.
British Institute Library, Barcelona.

In addition, I must express my thanks for the information or material provided by the writer Josep Maria Puigjaner, the former director of the Book Service of the Government of Catalonia; Father Josep Maria Blanquet, superior of the Congregation 'Fills de la Sagrada Família, Jesús, Maria i Josep'; Manuel Forasté, head of the Press Department of the Caixa de Catalunya Foundation; Father Jaume Aymar, Dean of the Ecclesiastical Faculty of Philosophy of Catalonia; Joan Francesc Mestre, of the Study Centre of Riudoms; Joan-Ramon Corts, Municipal Archivist of Riudoms; Montserrat Vilumara, niece of the architect Joan Bergós (1894-1974), who was a disciple of Gaudí; Francesc Jané, an erudite pharmacist of Esplugues de Llobregat; and Antoni M. Vidal Colomines, of the 'Amics de Gaudí' of Reus, a tireless disseminator of Gaudí's work throughout the world.

I am also indebted to all of those people who have provided me with data to complete and confirm the genealogy of the Cornet family; Josep Ballabriga, ex-mayor of Les Piles; the Tarragó family of Santa Coloma de Queralt; Josep M. Carreras Tarragó, a teacher, also of Santa Coloma de Queralt; and Mr. Vidal Colomines of Reus.

I must also recall here that the Cornet lineage was first studied, in the 1920's, by my great-uncle Gabriel Castellà i Raich, the archivist and historian of the town of Igualada.

This list would be incomplete if I did not mention my gratitude to Carles Duarte, a distinguished writer and member of the PEN Club, for having read certain chapters of this book and for his encouragement.

THE AUTHOR.